BN
3.60

W9-CUY-032

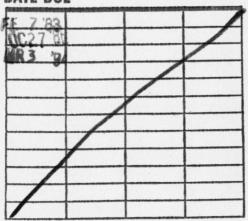

LAW AND MORALS

LAW AND MORALS

THE McNAIR LECTURES, 1923, DELIVERED AT THE UNIVERSITY OF NORTH CAROLINA

BY

ROSCOE POUND

CARTER PROFESSOR OF JURISPRUDENCE IN
HARVARD UNIVERSITY

ROTHMAN REPRINTS, Inc.
South Hackensack, New Jersey

AUGUSTUS M. KELLEY • PUBLISHERS
New York, New York
1969

First Published 1924

(Chapel Hill, N.C.: University of North Carolina Press)

Reprinted *1969* By

ROTHMAN REPRINTS, Inc.

57 Leuning Street

South Hackensack, New Jersey 07606

———

AUGUSTUS M. KELLEY · PUBLISHERS

24 East 22nd Street

New York, New York 10010

By Arrangement With

University of North Carolina Press

SBN *678 04532 1*

Library of Congress Catalogue Card Number

70-96339

Printed in the United States of America

TO

HENRY MOORE BATES

THE McNAIR LECTURES

The John Calvin McNair Lectures were founded through a bequest made by Rev. John Calvin McNair of the class of 1849 which became available to the University in 1906. The extract from the will referring to the foundation is as follows:

"As soon as the interest accruing thereon shall by said Trustees be deemed sufficient they shall employ some able scientific gentleman to deliver before the students then in attendance at said University, a course of lectures, the object of which lectures shall be to show the mutual bearing of science and theology upon each other, and to prove the existence of attributes (as far as may be) of God from nature. The lectures, which must be prepared by a member of some one of the evangelic denominations of christians, must be published within twelve months after delivery, either in pamphlet or book form."

PREFACE

Three subjects stand out in the juristic writing of the last century—the nature of law, the relation of law to morals, and the interpretation of legal history. The first was debated by the three nineteenth-century schools down to the end of the century. The second was debated by the analytical and the historical jurists, as against the eighteenth-century identification of the legal with the moral, and by the several types of the philosophical school, as between theories of subordination of jurisprudence to ethics and different theories of contrasting or opposing them. The third did not concern the analytical school. It was discussed by historical and by metaphysical jurists with reference to ethical and political interpretations. Later the mechanical sociologists argued for different types of ethnological and biological interpretation, while others, especially the economic realists, urged some form of economic interpretation. Both the controversies as to the nature of law and the interpretations of legal history are intimately related to the controversies as to the relation of law to morals. In a sense that relation was but one phase of the problem of the nature of law. Moreover the nature of law was involved in all interpretation of its development.

Today discussion of the nature of law is coming to be replaced by consideration of the end or purpose of law. Likewise the older discussions as to law and morals are coming to be merged in broader consideration of the place of law in the whole process of social control. And interpretation of legal history is ceasing to be debated on the hypothesis that there is some one simple idea upon which all the phenomena of law and of the history of law may be strung for every purpose and for all time. Yet the nineteenth-century discussions are far from having lost importance. We must work with the legal materials and with the juristic tools that are at hand, and we shall not understand those materials and their possibilities, nor shall we know the possibilities of those tools, except by critical study of the juristic thought of the immediate past.

Thus a history of juristic thought in the last century must precede an effective science of law for today; and one part of that history must be an account of juristic thought with respect to the relation of law to morals. But it must be remembered that this is only part of a larger story.

When presented as such, it must be to some extent a piece torn out of its setting in the whole. Nevertheless, if it is to be presented within the compass of a brief series of lectures, one must essay this tearing out process. And it is worth while to attempt to do so. For no small part of the task of the jurist of today is to appraise the value for present purposes of the science of law as it was in the last century. The first step in this appraisal must be to understand thoroughly the theories he is to appraise, and to do this he must apprehend the needs for which they were devised and their relation to the juristic problems of their time.

A complete treatment of the relation of law and morals would go into the social-philosophical and sociological theories of today no less elaborately than I have sought to go into the historical and analytical and metaphysical theories of the last century. But the limits of the series forbade. Moreover, the lesser task, to which alone the present lectures address themselves, is a necessary forerunner of adequate treatment of current theories.   R. P.

HARVARD LAW SCHOOL,
  March 31, 1923.

CONTENTS

LAW AND MORALS

I

THE HISTORICAL VIEW

If we compare the juristic writing and judicial decision of the end of the eighteenth century with juristic writing and judicial decision at the end of the nineteenth century, the entire change of front with respect to the nature of law, with respect to the source of the obligation of legal precepts, and with respect to the relation of law and morals and consequent relation of jurisprudence and ethics, challenges attention. Thus Blackstone[1] speaks of "ethics or natural law" as synonymous, and of natural law as the ultimate measure of obligation by which all legal precepts must be tried and from which they derive their whole force and authority.[2] Again Wilson's lectures on Law (delivered in 1790-1791 by one of the framers of the federal constitution and a justice of the Supreme Court of the United States) begin with a lecture on the moral basis of legal obligation and a lecture on the law of nature or

---

[1] 1 Bl. *Comm.* 41.

[2] "This law of nature, being co-eval with mankind and dictated by God himself, is, of course, superior to any other. It is binding all over the globe, in all countries and at all times; no human laws are of any validity, if contrary to this; and such of them as are valid derive all their force and all their validity mediately or immediately from this original." *Ibid.*

the universal moral principles of which positive laws are but declaratory.[3] In contrast, the institutional book of widest use in English-speaking lands at the end of the nineteenth century begins with an elaborate setting off of law from "all rules which, like the principles of morality . . . are enforced by an indeterminate authority" and conceives that natural law is wholly outside of the author's province.[4] Likewise Mr. Justice Miller, lecturing upon the constitution in 1889-1890, finds no occasion to speak of natural law nor of ethics but puts a political and historical foundation where Mr. Justice Wilson had put an ethical and philosophical foundation.[5] The same contrast appears, no less strikingly, if we compare eighteenth-century decisions on quasi contract or on the granting of new trials or on the interpretation of statutes with nineteenth-century decisions on the same subjects.[6] Yet the nine-

---

[3] 1 Wilson's Works (Andrews' ed.) 49-127.

[4] Holland, *Elements of Jurisprudence,* chaps. 3-4. Also compare with Blackstone the books now in use in England: Odgers, *The Common Law of England* (2 ed.) I, 2-3; Stephen, *Commentaries on the Laws of England* (16 ed. by Jenks) I, 11 ff.

[5] Miller, *Lectures on the Constitution of the United States,* Lect. 2, particularly pp. 82 ff.

[6] Compare the insistence upon honor and conscience in the old decisions on quasi contract—e.g., De Grey, C. J., in *Farmer v. Arundel,* 2 Wm. Bl. 824; Lord Mansfield, C. J., in *Bize v. Dickason,* 1 T. R. 285; De Grey, C. J., in *Jaques v. Golightly,* 2 Wm. Bl. 273 (not followed today); Lord Mansfield, C. J., in *Moses v. Macferian,* 2 Burr. 1005 (the result not law today);

teenth-century doctrines as to the nature of law, the obligation of legal precepts, and the relation of law and morals are intimately connected with the seventeenth and eighteenth-century doctrines on these points, in part as developments of different phases thereof, and in part as different forms of reaction therefrom, and in turn the natural-law doctrines have a like relation to theories that

---

Lord Loughborough, C. J., in *Jenkins v. Taylor,* 1 H. Bl. 90— with the complacent mechanical working out of an unjust result in *Baylis v. Bishop of London,* [1913] 1 Ch. 127.

As to the granting of new trials, compare *Deerly v. Duchess of Mazarine,* 2 Salk. 646; *Farewell v. Chaffey,* 1 Burr. 54; *Burton v. Thompson,* 2 Burr. 664, 665, with *Reg. v. Gibson,* 18 Q. B. D. 537, 540; *Waldron v. Waldron,* 156 U. S. 361, 380.

In *Deerly v. The Duchess of Mazarine* "the jury found for the plaintiff, though the Duchess gave good evidence of her coverture; and the court would not grant a new trial because there was no reason why the Duchess, who lived here as a feme sole, should set up coverture to avoid the payment of her just debts."

In *Reg. v. Gibson,* Lord Coleridge, C. J., says: "Until the passing of the Judicature Acts the rule was that if any bit of evidence not legally admissible, which might have affected the verdict, had gone to the jury, the party against whom it was given was entitled to a new trial, because the courts said that they would not weigh evidence. When, therefore, such evidence had gone to the jury a new trial was granted as a matter of right." So in *Waldron v. Waldron,* White, J., says: "It is elementary that the admission of illegal evidence, over objection, necessitates reversal."

As to the statute of limitations, compare *Trueman v. Fenton,* Cowp. 548, *Quantock v. England,* 5 Burr. 2630, with *Shapley v. Abbott,* 42 N. Y. 443. Undoubtedly in the two cases first cited Lord Mansfield carried his moral objections to the statute too far, ignoring other considerations that even a purely ethical view should not overlook. But at the other extreme the nineteenth-century decision is needlessly callous toward ethical considerations and proceeds upon a logical deduction from a form of words.

See also Willes, J., in *Miller v. Taylor,* 4 Burr. 2303, 2312 (1769) saying that "justice, moral fitness and public convenience . . . when applied to a new subject, make common law without a precedent," and compare Lord Macnaghten in *Blackburn v. Vigors,* 12 App. Cas. 531, 543 (1887).

4 LAW AND MORALS

had developed prior to the sixteenth century when
jurisprudence was but a branch or an application
of philosophical theology. Indeed the theological
basis of jurisprudence continued to be urged till
well into the nineteenth century.[7]

All discussion of the relation of law to morals,
of the relation of jurisprudence to ethics, goes
back to the Greek thinkers of the fifth century before Christ, who enquired whether the right or
the just was right and just by nature or only by
convention and enactment. In the Greek city-
state law was differentiating from a general social control as the normal and most efficacious
form thereof. Thus it attracted the attention of
thinkers as requiring a surer basis of obligation
than the mere habit of obedience or the mere will
of those who controlled political machinery for
the time being. The Greek philosopher noted
that while the phenomena of nature were uniform, the sun rose and set, fire burned and water
flowed in Greece, in Persia and at Carthage, on
the other hand, human laws and customs and ob-
servances were as diverse as possible, not only as
between Greeks and other peoples, but as between
the several Greek cities themselves, and even in

---

[7] 1 Bl. *Comm.* 40 ff.; 1 Wilson's Works (Andrews' ed.) 105
ff.; 1 Kent, *Comm.* 2; 1 Minor, *Institutes of Common and Statute
Law,* Intr. sect. ii.

the same city at different times.[8] Also he saw that this well known fact, tending to produce doubt as to the binding force of legal precepts, and to make them appear something subject to the arbitrary power of oligarchy or of demos, according as the one or the other was politically dominant for the moment, endangered the general security. The old-time explanations that law was the gift of a god,[9] or the teaching of the wise men who knew the good old customs acceptable to the gods,[10] or the more modern explanation that it was something to which all the citizens had agreed, binding therefore with the sanctity of a formal promise,[11] did not satisfy in the contests between the aristocracy and the mass of the low born, in the struggles of the demos to hold in check masterful god-descended individuals with scant respect for humanly imposed restrictions upon their god-given powers, and in the competition between the remnants of a class tradition

---

[8] Pseudo-Plato, *Minos,* 315 B, 315 C, 316 A; Aristotle, *Nicomachaean Ethics,* v, 7. Plato, *Protagoras,* 337 D; Archelaus, ap. Diog. Laert. ii, 16. Cf. Cicero, *De Republica,* iii.

[9] Demosthenes, *Against Aristogeiton,* 774; Cicero, *Philippic.* xi, 12, 28. Compare Heraclitus on law, Diels, *Fragmente der Vorsokratiker,* fr. 44.

[10] Demosthenes, *Against Aristogeiton,* 774. Or that it was a body of tried customs of immemorial antiquity. Pseudo-Plato, *Minos,* 321 B, 321 C; Plato, *Laws,* 797 D.

[11] Demosthenes, *Against Aristogeiton,* 774; Plato, *Crito,* 50 C, 51 D, 52 D; Pseudo-Plato, *Minos,* 314 C; Xenophon, *Memorabilia,* 1, 2, § 43; Anaximenes, quoted by Aristotle, *Rhetoric to Alexander,* i.

and the tendency to substitute arbitrary enact-
ments established by legislative fiat at the instance
of a demagogue.[12]   Hence the philosopher sought
to find a foundation for assured security of the
social order through the analogy of the constancy
and universality of the everyday phenomena of
physical nature, exactly as the positivist sociologists today seek to find general laws of social
phenomena of the same sort, and to be discovered
in the same way, as the laws of physics or of
astronomy.[13]   But the time was not ripe for a
natural science of the social and legal order in
the modern sense of "natural," and the attempt
to distinguish between the permanent and the
transitory in social control could be made only
from the standpoint of a metaphysical ethics.

In the hands of Roman lawyers, the Greek
theories of what was right by nature and what
was right by convention or enactment gave rise
to a distinction between law by nature and law by
custom or enactment.   For the growing point of
Roman law, when it came in contact with Greek
philosophy, ~was in the opinions and writings of
the jurisconsults, who had no formal lawmaking

---

[12] Plato, *Laws,* 797 D.
[13] Durkheim, *Les règles de la méthode sociologique* (6 ed.) 176-
179; Lévy-Bruhl, *La morale et la science des moeurs* (5 ed.)
285 ff.

authority. Their opinions had to maintain themselves on the basis of their intrinsic reasonableness. As the Greeks would have put it, they were
law, if at all, by nature rather than by custom or
enactment. The right or the just by nature became law by nature or natural law, and thus begins the identification of the legal with the moral
that has been characteristic of natural-law thinking ever since.[14]

To the later Middle Ages Aristotle and Justinian were authorities to be interpreted only.
Hence the doctrine of natural law, set forth by
these authorities, was received, without any reception of the creative method or critical measur-
ing of legal precepts by moral standards which it
implied. For the Middle Ages did not need a
creative theory as such. On the one hand, there
was need of a stabilizing theory, after centuries
of disorder. On the other hand, there was need
of a general law to supersede, or to eke out and
give a new start and better guidance to, the local
laws and customs which were proving inadequate

[14] Note how Cicero seeks to expound the concrete content of
natural law. E.g., *De officiis*, i, 7, 20-23; i, 10, 32; i, 13; i, 41,
148; iii, 13-17; iii, 25. Note also the way in which the ethical
conception of a moral duty was taken over into the law as a
duty of good faith in view of the nature of one's undertaking and
thus became a legal duty. E.g., compare Cicero, *De officiis*, iii,
17, 70, and Cicero, *De natura deorum*, iii, 30, 74, with Gaius, iv,
§ 62 and *Inst.* iv. 6, § 30.

in the progress of society. Authority—the inevitable logical development of unchallengeable texts
—supplied the one need; so-called interpretation
of Roman law supplied the other. Natural law
was proclaimed by the authoritative books and so
was received. But a philosophical-theological
foundation was put under it. It proceeded immediately from reason but ultimately from God.
It was a reflection of the "reason of the divine
wisdom governing the whole universe."[15] Thus
natural law for a season was used as a prop to
authority rather than as a means of shaking it.[16]

In the revolt against authority at the Reformation, the Protestant jurist-theologians eliminated
the theological side of medieval natural law and
sought to put it once more squarely on the basis
of reason. But Grotius, starting out by adopting

---

[15] "A rule of law is nothing else than a dictate of practical
reason in the ruler who governs a perfect society. But supposing
that the world is ruled by divine Providence, it is manifest that
the whole society of the universe is governed by divine reason.
Hence the plan of governing things as it exists in God the ruler
of the universe, has the character of law. . . This manner
of law must be called eternal. . . Since all things subject to divine
Providence are ruled and measured by the eternal law, it is
manifest that they all participate in the eternal law to some
extent. . . But . . . the rational creature is subject to
divine Providence in a more excellent way, being itself a par-
taker in Providence. Hence it has a participation in the eternal
law. . . Such participation in the eternal law on the part of a
rational creature is called natural law." Thomas Aquinas, *Summa
Theologiae,* i-ii, qu. 91, art. 1-2. See id. qu. 93, art. 1-3, 6.

[16] See Figgis, *Studies of Political Thought from Gerson to
Grotius,* 7-8.

this divorce of jurisprudence from theology,[17] reverts to the theological and puts the natural law from which the law of the state derives all its force and validity upon two bases: (1) eternal reason, and (2)) the will of God who wills only reason.[18] The same twofold basis may be seen in Blackstone.[19] Yet with all these writers the real foundation is manifestly rational. As Hemmingsen put it, reason may show us the whole of their scheme of natural law "without the prophetic and apostolic voice."[20] Accordingly Mr. Justice Wilson tells us, by way of explanation, that God "is under the glorious necessity of not contradicting himself"[21] and thus of conforming to the exigencies of human reason. As the scholastic theologians had set out to convince and convert the infidel and the heretic by sheer force of reason, the natural-law jurists, in an age of scepticism, were eager to convince all men upon an unimpeachable basis of reason and thus secure a general adherence to the precepts of the legal order.

---

[17] *De jure belli ac pacis, prolegomena,* § 11.

[18] Id. § 12.

[19] 1 Bl. *Comm.* 42.

[20] *De lege naturae apodictica methodus,* preface; Kaltenborn, *Die Vorläufer des Hugo Grotius,* II, 43.

[21] 1 Wilson's Works (Andrews' ed.) 124.

In the nineteenth-century the matter came to be put in a wholly different way. Down to Kant at the end of the eighteenth century positive law or conventional right, on the one hand, had been contrasted with a body of ideal moral and hence legal precepts—natural law—on the other hand. Kant instead set over against positive law the immutable principles of positive legislation—the principles of making positive law.[22] This is not natural law in the seventeenth and eighteenth-century sense. It is not a body of moral and hence legal precepts which is law in the same sense as the positive law only in a higher form. He thinks rather of certain eternal, immutable principles governing the making of law, by which law and lawmaking must be judged. Kant wrote before the historical school, at a time when legal institutions and systems of positive law as well as single legal rules and doctrines were regarded as products of human wisdom.[23] But his

---

[22] *"Rechtslehre* is the aggregate of the rules of right for which an external lawmaking is possible. . . *Rechtswissenschaft* means the systematic knowledge of natural *Rechtslehre.* It is from this science that the immutable principles of all positive legislation must be derived by practical jurists and lawgivers." Kant, *Metaphysische Anfangsgründe der Rechtslehre,* Introduction, § A (1797).

[23] E.g., Dr. Johnson said that "the law is the last result of human wisdom acting upon human experience for the benefit of the public." Boswell, *Life of Johnson* (Croker ed., 1859) II, 258. Compare Hale's view as to the statutory origin of the common law, *History of the Common Law,* 3-4, 67-68. See also Croce, *Storia della storiografia Italiana nel secolo decimonono,* I, 22-23.

is not in truth a creative theory. It belongs rather to the next century in which more and more law was thought of, not as a product of wisdom, but as a spontaneous evolution. It is a critical theory. He does not find an ultimate pattern code of rules with reference whereto we may make new positive precepts with confidence. He finds ultimate principles of criticism by which we may criticize what we have already. All that he has in common with the philosophical jurisprudence of his predecessors is a belief that he can find something eternal and immutable on which the law may be rested. But that something is quite different from what the classical jurists of the law-of-nature school had been finding, and is reached in another way. He begins with the conscious free-willing individual man as an ultimate metaphysical datum. He finds an ultimate principle of right by deduction from a rational harmonizing of free wills,[24] not a body of principles of right by deduction from the ideal of the abstract man as a moral creature. Thus he deduces a principle of right and law by which all

---

[24] "Acts of will or voluntary choice are thus regarded only in so far as they are free and as to whether the action of one can harmonize with the will of another according to a universal law. Right, therefore, includes the whole of the conditions under which the voluntary actions of any one person may be harmonized in reality with the voluntary actions of every other person according to a universal law of freedom." *Metaphysische Anfangsgründe der Rechtslehre,* Introduction, § B, 3.

things legal may be measured and justified. In consequence natural law entered upon a new era, comparable to the natural law of the later Middle Ages. It was used no longer to break down the authority of received legal materials, nor to bring in new materials from outside of the law by identifying law and morals, nor to create law. It became instead a means of upholding and justifying and systematizing the existing legal order. The subordination of law to morals and of jurisprudence to ethics was given up.[25]

Note how we have now come back to the point from which we set out. The Greeks put a theoretical moral foundation under law by the doctrine of natural rights. The Roman jurists made natural right into natural law and sought to discover the content of this natural law and to declare it. Thus they gave us an ethical philosophical natural law with an ideal form of Roman legal precepts, shaped with reference to an ideal of the existing social order, for its chief content. The Middle Ages put a theological foundation under natural law, giving us an authoritative theological natural law, which was

---

[25] E.g., note the distinction between jurisprudence and ethics in the introduction to the *Rechtslehre*, § C. As to the effect of this upon English analytical jurisprudence, see Pound, *Interpretations of Legal History*, 98-99.

used to sustain the Roman law, as interpreted by the glossators and commentators, in the process of receiving it as the law of Continental Europe. The seventeenth and eighteenth centuries took out this theological foundation and replaced it or partially replaced it by a rational foundation, giving us a rational-theological or rational-ethical natural law, which was used to make the strict law of the glossators and commentators and the feudal land law of medieval England into systems of law for the modern world. At the end of the eighteenth century Kant replaced the rational foundation by a metaphysical foundation, giving us a metaphysical natural law used to demonstrate the obligatory force of the legal order as it is. It remained only for the analytical jurists to argue that no foundation was needed; to urge that so far as concerns judge or jurist the law stands upon its own basis as a system of precepts imposed or enforced by the sovereign. If we felt inclined to go outside of the body of legal precepts so imposed or enforced, they referred us to the science of politics.[26] Presently the analytical school in politics in America carried the

---

[26] "The philosophical analysis and definition of law belongs, in our judgment, neither to the historical nor to the dogmatic science of law, but to the theoretical part of politics." Pollock in Pollock and Maitland, *History of English Law* (1 ed.) I, xxiii (1895). Compare Pollock, *Oxford Lectures*, 14 (1890).

movement for casting out ethics still further and limited the science of politics to a descriptive analytical method, leaving what ought to be to the philosophers as such. Thus the cycle is complete. We are back to the state as the unchallengeable authority behind legal precepts. The state takes the place of Jehovah handing the tables of the law to Moses, or Manu dictating the sacred law, or the Sun-god handing the code to Hammurabi. Law is law by convention and enactment—the proposition, plausibly maintained by sophists, which led Greek philosophers to seek some basis that made a stronger appeal to men to uphold the legal order and the security of social institutions.[27]

Already at the end of the eighteenth century natural-law thinking had divided into two channels. The one led to a purely justifying and explanatory use of natural law; to a philosophical jurisprudence which gave specious ex post facto reasons for a settled system of positive legal precepts, regarded as an authoritative exposition of the ideal natural law of which in theory all posi-

---

[27] Archelaus, quoted by Diogenes Laertius, ii, 16; Plato, *Protagoras*, 337 D; Pseudo-Plato, *Minos*, 314 B-314 E. Compare Xenophon, *Memorabilia*, iv, 4, 14. See Vinogradoff, *Historical Jurisprudence*, II, 31-42.

tive law was but declaratory.[28]   Thinking of
positive law as declaratory and of the declaration
as an effort of human reason, it stressed the authoritative nature of the reason that had ascer-
tained and declared the law, at the expense of
the reasons that would question or criticize it.
This way of thinking marks the transition from
the creative natural law of the seventeenth and
eighteenth centuries, when the law of the world
of today was remaking out of the strict law of
the Middle Ages, to the maturity of law with its
insistence upon security of acquisitions and security of transactions and hence upon the rule of
property as the type of all legal precepts.   The
other kept to insistence upon the positive law as
declaratory; but in a time when a creative theory
was no longer required led to a conception of legal
precepts as declaratory, not of ideal moral precepts, but of customs evolved in the experience
of life in civilized society.   Thus the declaration
or promulgation was not an act of creation.   It
was a formal recognition of what existed as law
already—not as an ideal moral rule, binding be-

---

[28] Hegel refers to this as "the fraud which is inseparably involved in the method of the understanding and its arguings,
namely, giving a good reason for a bad thing and assuming that
in that way one has justified it."   *Grundlinien der Philosophie
des Rechts* (3 ed.) 29.   For a striking example see *Hyatt v.
Adams*, 16 Mich. 180, 191-192 and the comments in Cooley,
Torts (1 ed.) 26-28.

cause of its intrinsic moral authority, but as a
custom of popular action having its roots in the
very spirit of the people.[29]

Although the historical school overthrew the
natural-law jurisprudence of the eighteenth century, its connection therewith is immediate and
palpable. It rejected the conception that positive
law was made by human wisdom. The law-of-
nature school held that natural law was to be
discovered but was immutable and eternal. When
it was discovered, however, positive law might be
and ought to be made consciously and deliberately
in its image. The historical school agreed that
there was something not made by human wisdom
which was behind positive law. But they held that
positive law itself was only to be found. It could
not be made. When men seemed to make it, the
work of their hands was futile except as it
declared or put in better form what existed already in human experience and not merely as an
ideal.[30] Under the influence of Hegel, law came
to be thought of as an unfolding or a realizing of

---

[29] Savigny, *System des heutigen römischen Rechts,* I, § 7
(1840).

[30] "One might wish to assume that law has a wholly variable
origin, according to the influence of chance or of human will or
deliberation or wisdom. But this assumption contradicts the undoubted fact that everywhere, when a relation of right and law
comes in question or men become conscious of it, a rule therefor
is already at hand and hence it is neither necessary nor possible to invent it for the first time." *Ibid.*

the idea of right. Legal history was a record of
how the idea of right had realized itself pro-
gressively in human experience of the administration of justice.[31] Thus for a time the historical
school kept up a certain relation of jurisprudence
to ethics. But before long the ethical interpretation gave way to a political interpretation. An
idea of freedom took the place of the idea of
right.[32] Ethical considerations were banished
from historical jurisprudence.[33]

To the historical school the jurist is observing
or studying the realization of the idea of right, or
of the idea of freedom, in experience in society,
and the unconscious or spontaneous formulations
of that experience in general moral sentiment, in
customs of popular action, and in customs of
judicial decision. They saw clearly that the
formal legal precept as such by no means did the
whole work of administering justice; that there
was something else, that entered decisively into
all the work of tribunals, that was not to be
found in the texts of codes or statutes. The

---

[31] See Pound, *Interpretations of Legal History*, 22-23, 25-49.

[32] Puchta, *Cursus der Institutionen*, § 2 (1841); Lorimer, *Institutes of Law*, (2 ed.) 354-355 (1880); Carter, *Law: Its Origin, Growth and Function*, 336-337 (1906). See Pound, *Interpretations of Legal History*, 45-68.

[33] Maine, *Early History of Institutions*, lect. 12 (1874). See Lord Russell, *International Law*, 19 Rep. Am. Bar Assn. 253, 268 (1896).

natural-law jurists had seen this also and had identified the unexpressed something with an eternal, ideal system of moral and hence legal principles which the positive law could but imperfectly reflect. The historical jurists identified this decisive but unexpressed element with habit and custom,[34] which in turn they traced back to the spirit of the people and thence metaphysically to the idea realizing itself in and through that spirit.[35] But they thought of this element in terms of customs of popular action and of human intercourse in civilized society, and thus ignored the chief factor in judicial and juristic shaping of legal precepts, namely, habits of thought as to what comports with an ideal of the end of law and of a system of legal precepts in view thereof. The natural-law theory comes much nearer to describing this element in what we call "the law" than the historical theory of "custom."

Orthodox historical jurisprudence of the nineteenth century rejected all creative participation of judge or jurist or lawgiver in the making or even the real formulation of the law. It conceived

---

[34] Clark, *Practical Jurisprudence*, 151, 331-332 (1883); Carter, *The Ideal and the Actual in Law*, 10-11 (1890); Jenks, *Law and Politics in the Middle Ages*, 56-63 (1897); Rattigan, *Science of Jurisprudence*, § 72 (1899); Bryce, *Studies in History and Jurisprudence*, 640, 672-673 (1901). Compare Ehrlich, *Grundlegung der Soziologie des Rechts*, 352-380.

[35] See Pound, *Interpretations of Legal History*, lects. I-III.

that the judge was neither the molder of the legal precept nor the agency by which it was given effect. He but recognized it. The precept was given its real force by the "social standard of justice." It was found and given technical expression by the court in its search for the binding rule.[36] It was obligatory because of its intrinsic force as an expression of a principle of action discovered by human experience, and that experience, in turn, was significant because it involved the realization of an idea.[37]

Thus "custom" took the place which morals had held in the juristic thought of the two preceding centuries. But when the nineteenth-century jurists spoke of "custom" they meant more than one thing. They used the term customary law to in-

---

[36] Carter, *The Ideal and the Actual in Law*, 10-11 (1890).

[37] "Right and law are a product of the will of the people. But a people only wills what expresses its stage of civilization and its needs for the time being. Therefore right and law develop in space and time. They have a history because they are human facts, a history, that is, in the sense of 'an unfolding of its nature in which it maintains its identity unchanged.' Hence to understand the present position of a people in its legal life, and in order to perceive what it must will with respect to right and law, an adequate investigation of its history is required. Now since every people has a share in the development of right and law and here as in all other respects it gives us a picture of humanity in miniature, it follows that right is living in every people but complete in all peoples." Friedländer, *Juristiche Encyklopädie*, 65 (1847).
"A positive law in its widest sense may be defined as the expression of the idea of right involved in the relation of two or more human beings." Miller, *Lectures on the Philosophy of Law*, 9 (1884).

clude three distinct types of legal precept, looked
at with respect to their source: (1) law formulated through custom of popular action, such as
the older mining law of our western states, or the
older law merchant, (2) law formulated through
customs of judicial decision, such as the bulk of
Anglo-American common law, (3) law formulated through doctrinal writing and scientific discussion of legal principles, such as the civil law
(or as it is called on its own ground, the common law) of Continental Europe.[38]   In the writings of the historical school customs of judicial
decision and traditional lines of doctrinal writing
were treated as if they were but examples of or
reflections of customs of popular action, even
though it might well be that they derived from
Greek philosophical speculation,[39] or from the
legal problems of republican Rome,[40] or from

[38] See Clark, *Roman Private Law: Jurisprudence,* I, §§ 7-8,
particularly pp. 348-351, 403, 407-413.

[39] E.g., the rules as to border trees.   See Aristotle, *Hist. Animal.* v, 1; Aristotle, *Meteorol.* iv, 8; *Digest,* xxix, 2, 9, § 2, xli, 1,
26, § 1; *Inst.* ii, 1, 31; *Bracton,* fol. 10; *Waterman v. Soper,* 1
Ld. Raym. 737; *Anon.* 2 Rolle, 255.   But the settled rule is now
otherwise at common law, if it is known on which side of the
line the tree was planted.   See also Sokolowski, *Philosophie im
Privatrecht,* I, 148 ff.

[40] E.g., the rule in equity as to legacies on impossible or illegal
conditions precedent.   *Lowther v. Cavendish,* 1 Eden, 99 (1758);
Brown v. Peck 1 Eden, 140 (1758); *In re Haight's Will,* 51 App.
Div. 310.   See Pound, *Legacies on Impossible or Illegal Conditions Precedent,* 3 Ill. Law Rev. 1, 4-6.

scholastic subtleties of the Middle Ages,[41] and
though it happened often that the traditional
course of judicial decision or of doctrinal thought
and the customary course of popular thought on a
given point were wholly at variance.[42] For the
historical jurist assumed without question the
truth of a mode of juristic speech that had prevailed since the seventeenth century. In the later
Middle Ages the academic theory of the statutory
binding force of the legislation of Justinian as
the law of the "empire" passed over to the courts,
and it had become accepted by the sixteenth century. In the seventeenth century it was definitely
demonstrated that the academic theory could not
be maintained and that Roman law obtained in
the courts simply because it had been received in
the custom of tribunals. If one thought philo-
sophically, he said that it had the authority of

---

[41] E.g., the rules of limitation of estates at common law, derived logically from a theory as to abeyance of seisin. Challis,
Law of Real Property, chap. 11. Compare the later rules allowing limitations which were not possible at common law to be
made indirectly through uses.

[42] Examples may be seen in the American common law as to
corporations in comparison with the ideas of business men—see
Machen, *Do the Incorporation Laws Allow Sufficient Freedom to
Industrial Enterprise?*, Rep. Maryland Bar Assn., XIV, 78, 81-84,
85, 87-89 (1909); *People* v. *Shedd*, 241 Ill. 155 (1909),—and in
the common-law conception of partnership in comparison with
the business man's conception—see Brannan, *The Separate Estates of Non-Bankrupt Partners*, 20 Harv. Law Rev. 589, 593;
Crane, *The Uniform Partnership Act*, 28 Harv. Law Rev. 762,
765-766. See also Austin, *Jurisprudence* (Student's edition)
272-273; Clark, *Roman Private Law: Jurisprudence*, I, 383, 407-
408.

embodied reason.[43]. It was the culmination of rational discovery and declaration of natural law. If one thought juristically, he said that it had the authority of long usage which, as the Roman texts themselves told us, stood legally upon the same plane with enacted rule.[44] All that was not legislative in origin was called customary law. But during the reign of the legislative theory of Roman law the Germanic law in Western Europe had been contrasted therewith as customary law and, indeed, the written laws of the Germanic peoples were but declaratory of customs in a stage in which religious usage, social customs and traditional modes of decision make up an undifferentiated body of precepts of social control. As men thought with respect to these precepts, the basis of their authority was that long usage had proved them acceptable to God.[45] Hence both elements of the common law could be called customary, and if one accepted legal dogmatic fictions at par, it seemed that the common law of all civilized countries at bottom rested upon cus-

---

[43] "The grand destinies of Rome are not yet accomplished; she reigns throughout the world by her reason after having ceased to reign by her authority." D'Aguesseau (1668-1751) transl. by Kent, *Commentaries,* I, 516.

[44] *Inst.* i, 2, § 9; Dig. i, 3, 32, § 1.

[45] See Jenks, *Law and Politics in the Middle Ages,* 56-57; Heusler, *Institutionen des Deutschen Privatrechts,* I, 1.

toms of popular action. Customs grew; they were not made to order. Therefore law also grew; it was not made. The function of legislation was only to "restate," to promulgate, to give a better ordered, systematically arranged statement, reconciling incidental inconsistencies. Behind these promulgations or restatements was the real law, evolving spontaneously through the inherent power of the idea. All attempts at conscious interference with its spontaneous evolution were simply futile. History replaced ethical philosophy as the explanation of the universal element to which positive legal precepts were approximating and by which they were to be judged.

It has been remarked more than once that the historical jurist merely gave us a new natural law on a new basis.[46] He, too, found universal ideal principles to which positive law must conform. But they were not principles of morals. They were principles of customary action. They were not demonstrated by reason. They were discovered by historical study. They did not admit of formulation in a perfect code through the activity of master-reasoners. They formulated themselves in experience of affairs and in experience

---

[46] E.g., Bekker, *Recht des Besitzes*, 3; Neukamp, *Einleitung in eine Entwickelungsgeschichte des Rechts*, 28-29.

of administering justice. The moral, as such, was quite out of the domain of judge and jurist.[47]

When we consider the relation between law and morals much depends upon what we mean by "law." At one extreme the analytical jurist means the aggregate of authoritative legal precepts that are applied by tribunals as such in a given time and place.[48] At the other extreme, the historical jurist is apt to think of the history of all social control as the history of law.[49] Hence where the analytical jurist thinks of an authoritative precept as established and enforced by some agency of politically organized society, the historical jurist thinks of a customary precept, with

---

[47] "The law was held to be something essentially out of the domain of the operation of conscious, voluntary human mind, since it was but the manifestation of the spirit of the people realizing the reasonable for the time being. Hence the science of law shrunk to a purely theoretical working over of historical data, excluding all values. Speculation as to a law that ought to be, over and distinguished from a body of actual law, was rejected as unscientific dreaming. And as a consequence, the founder of the school denied to his age the vocation for legislation, with arguments which would hold for every time, if they were but sound." Kantorowicz, *Zur Lehre vom richtigen Recht,* 8 (1909). See Pollock, *Essays in Jurisprudence and Ethics,* 25-26 (1882).

[48] "Now *law* or *the law,* taken indefinitely, is an abstract and collective term; which, when it means anything, can mean neither more nor less than the sum total of a number of individual laws taken together." Bentham, *Principles of Morals and Legislation,* 324 (1789). See Austin, *Jurisprudence,* lect. I (1832); Holland, *Jurisprudence,* chaps. 2-3 (1880).

[49] Maine, *Early History of Institutions,* lect. 13 (1874); Vinogradoff, *Historical Jurisprudence,* I, 157-159. "I should say that any rules of human conduct actually obtaining among any considerable number of human beings, in some manner connected or associated together by virtue of human sanctions, might not improperly be called positive law." Clark, *Roman Private Law: Jurisprudence,* I, 90.

an origin wholly independent of politically organized society; recognized and given effect in a course of judicial action. The former sees chiefly the force and constraint behind legal rules. He conceives that the sanction of law is enforcement by the judicial and administrative organs of the state and that nothing which lacks that direct and immediate backing of organized force is law.[50] The historical jurist, on the other hand, sees chiefly the social pressure behind legal rules. He finds sanction in habits of obedience, displeasure of one's fellow men, public sentiment or opinion, or the social standard of justice.[51]

In truth the different schools of jurists in the last century were looking primarily at distinct elements of the complex aggregate that we call "law."[52] The analytical jurist thought exclusively of the body of established precepts whereby a definite legal result is attached to a definite state of facts. The historical jurist was likely to think exclusively of the body of traditional ideas

---

[50] Gray, *Nature and Sources of the Law* (2 ed.) 94-95; Holland, *Jurisprudence,* chap. 3; Anson, *Law and Custom of the Constitution,* I, 8; Salmond, *Jurisprudence,* § 5; Clark, *Roman Private Law: Jurisprudence,* I, 75.

[51] Maine, *International Law,* lect. 2 (1888); Westlake, *International Law,* I, 7 (1910); Clark, *Practical Jurisprudence,* 134 (1883); Lightwood, *The Nature of Positive Law,* 389 (1883); Carter, *The Ideal and the Actual in Law,* 10-11 (1890).

[52] See Pound, *The Theory of Judicial Decision,* 36 Harv. Law Rev. 641, 644-657.

as to how causes should be decided, and the traditional technique of developing and applying those ideas, by which legal precepts are eked out, extended, restricted and adapted to the exigencies of life. The philosophical jurist looked chiefly, if not exclusively, at a third element, namely, a body of philosophical-political and ethical ideas as to the end of law and as to what legal precepts should be in view thereof, with reference to which, consciously or unconsciously, legal precepts and traditional principles of decision and the traditional technique are continually being reshaped and given new content and new application. The philosophical jurist has called this third element "natural law" and has given us a theory of all law on the basis thereof. The historical jurist has called the second element "custom" and has given us a theory of all law on that basis. The analytical jurist has sought to treat the second and third elements as but sources from which legal precepts are drawn or raw materials from which legal precepts are made, but which are themselves no part of the law, and so has given us a theory of law exclusively in terms of the first element. These different views, laying stress upon different elements in the whole mass of materials upon which judicial decision proceeds, respond to different demands made upon juristic thought in different stages of legal development.

Today the legal order is the most conspicuous and most effective form of social control. All other agencies of social control operate under the scrutiny, and in subordination to the exigencies, of the law. Religion, the internal discipline of the group of kindred or its analogues, and social customs, which were the efficient agencies of social control in antiquity, have gradually yielded their leadership as regulative systems to the claims of politically organized society. But in the beginnings of legal development, in what we may call the pre-legal stage or the stage of primitive law, religion, law and morals are undifferentiated in a simpler social control that precedes the rise of the political organization at the expense of kin organization and of religious organization. As late as the fourth century before Christ, after the. city-state had achieved a high degree of political development, the Greek word νόμος, which we translate as "law," was used indiscriminately, often by the same author, to mean traditional religious usage or observance, traditional social custom, traditional moral ideas, law (or rather social control) in general, and a par-

ticular enacted legal precept.[53] We must remember that the first legislation is but publication
of received tradition. Hence the analytical line
between social control through customs of popular action, through precepts declaring those customs, and through enacted rules, made unconsciously at first in the belief that they are but
publications, then made consciously under a fiction of declaring custom, and at length made deliberately as new rules—this line is long imper-
ceptible and is only gradually admitted. In the
pseudo-Platonic Minos, Socrates speaks of a
gardener's manual as the laws of gardening and
of a cook book as the laws of cookery,[54] since
the settled customs and crystallized traditional
experience and formulated precepts of gardeners
and cooks seemed on exactly the same plane as
the customs and crystallized experience and
formulated precepts as to conduct in relations of
man with man that made up what we now call
the law.

---

[53] As the whole of social control: Plato, *Hippias Major*, 284;
Plato, *Protagoras*, 337 D; Aristotle, *Politics*, 1287 A. As ethical
custom: Pseudo-Plato, *Minos*, 513 D. Referring to funeral
ceremonies required by religious custom: See Dareste, *Les
plaidoyers politiques de Démosthène*, II, 3, II, 20. As a traditional or customary ethical principle: Aristotle, *Politics*, 1287 B.
As a moral precept: See Dareste, *Les plaidoyers politiques de
Démosthène*, II, 329, 344 (cf. Ulpian in Inst. i, 1, 4, Dig. i, 1, 1,
§ 3). Referring to conventions as opposed to "nature:" Democri-
tus, quoted by Sextus Empiricus, *Math.* vii, 135; Plato, *Gorgias*,
483-484. As a rule of law: Aristotle, *Politics*, 1286 A, 1287 A,
1287 B.

[54] 316 C—317B. The whole argument turns on the undifferentiated multiplicity of meanings of νόμος.

We begin, then, with a condition of undifferentiated social control—as we should have said in
the last century, a condition of undifferentiated
religion, morals and law—in which law, as we
now think of it, that is, social control through the
force of politically organized society, is the least
in scope and the least in efficacy of the three.
When we first know the Roman law not only do
fas (what accords with the will of the gods) and
boni mores (what accords with the social customs
of men) bear most of the burden of social control, but their sanctions, the fear of the super-
natural and the power of devotion of transgres-
sors to the infernal gods, of sacrificial execution
and of excommunication, and the kin or guild
discipline on the basis of reprehending things
that "are not done," are much stronger than the
relatively feeble enforcing machinery of the *ius
ciuile* (that which accords with the custom or the
declared will of the state). Such matters as good
faith in transactions, keeping promises, perform-
ing agreements, are left to religion and morals
rather than committed to the law, and when the
law gradually takes them over they long retain
the form given to them by religion. Thus it could
be said that law and morals have a common
origin but diverge in their development.

This divergence becomes marked when we pass to the next stage in the development of legal systems, the stage of the strict law. In this stage the state or politically organized society has definitely prevailed, and law in the sense of the analytical jurist has been definitely set off from other agencies of social control. But legal precepts in this stage are crude and rigid. The law is a system of remedies and its rules are chiefly procedural, defining in a hard and fast manner the cases in which tribunals will interfere and the way in which they will interfere. From the standpoint of the relation of law and morals, this is a stage of codified or crystallized custom which in time is outstripped by morality and does not possess sufficient power of growth to keep abreast. Ancient codes and bodies of formulated customary law, which are the basis of the legal system in the strict law, are made up of definite, precise, detailed provisions for simple, exact states of fact. In this stage reliance is had upon rule and form to insure certainty and thus to maintain the general security. There are no generalizations and the premises are not broad enough to allow of growth by interpretation outside of narrow limits. For example, interpretation of the Twelve Tables could not provide a better order of in-

heritance, based on blood relationship, when the
order of the strict law, based on the old house-
hold organization and ancestor-worship, ceased to
accord with the moral ideas of the time. No development of common-law property ideas could
give effect to the purely moral obligation of the
trustee. No development of common-law writs,
as they took fixed form after the thirteenth century, could give equitable relief for fraud. And
so at the end of this stage the law had come to
be highly unmoral. It regarded nothing but conformity or want of conformity to its forms and
rules. The moral aspect of situations, the moral
aspects of conduct were wholly indifferent. Both
in Roman law and in our own law the ideas of
this stage gave a direction to thinking about law
which persisted into the succeeding stages. The
old treatises on the *ius ciuile,* or strict law of the
Roman city, and the writings of Sir Edward
Coke in our law,[55] each coming at the end of a

---

[55] "Our student shall observe, that the knowledge of the law
is like a deepe well, out of which each man draweth according to
the strength of his understanding. He that reacheth deepest, he
seeth the amiable and admirable secrets of the law, wherein I
assure you the sages of the law in former times (whereof sir William Herle was a principall one) have had the deepest reach. And
as the bucket in the depth is easily drawn to the uppermost part
of the water, (for *nullum elementum in suo proprio loco est
grave*) but take it from the water, it cannot be drawne up but
with great difficultie; so albeit beginnings of this study seem
difficult, yet when the professor of the law can dive into the
depth, it is delightfull easie and without any heavy burthen so
long as he keepe himselfe in his own proper element." *Co. Litt.*
71 a.

stage of the strict law and summing up the achievements of that stage as the basis for a new start, imposed something of the spirit of the strict law upon each system for times to come, and are in large part responsible for a certain conviction that the positive law is of necessity unmoral or must inevitably ignore moral considerations—a conviction which is marked in the legal science of the last century.

In a third stage of legal development there is a large infusion into the law of purely moral ideas from without. This is a stage of growth, and growth in law takes place chiefly by assimilation and adaptation of materials drawn from other legal systems or from outside of the law. At Rome in the classical period Greek ethical philosophy was drawn upon. In England in the rise of the court of chancery and development of equity, ethical ideas from the casuist literature

---

"For reason is the life of the law, nay the common law itselfe is nothing else but reason; which is to be understood of an artificiall perfection of reason, gotten by long study, observation, and experience, and not of every man's naturall reason; for, *Nemo nascitur artifex.*" *Co. Litt.* 97 b.

"Then the King said that he thought the law was founded upon reason, and that he and others had reason as well as the judges: to which it was answered by me that true it was, that God had endowed his Majesty with excellent science, and great endowments of nature; but his Majesty was not learned in the laws of his realm of England, and causes which concern the life, or inheritance, or goods or fortunes of his subjects, are not to be decided by natural reason, but by the artificial reason and judgment of law, which law is an art which requires long study and experience before that a man can attain to the cognizance of it." *Prohibitions del Roy,* 12 Rep. 63, 64.

of the sixteenth century,[56] and the general notions
of right and wrong held by chancellors who were
not common-law lawyers, were made liberalizing
agencies. In Continental Europe of the seventeenth and eighteenth centuries the philosophical
ideas of juristic writers upon the law of nature
were used in the same way. Thus moral duty
was turned into legal duty and put in the fore-
ground in place of legal remedy. Reason was re-
lied upon rather than strict rule. The individual
human being, as the moral unit, became the legal
unit. It was conceived that the moral principle,
simply as such and for that reason, was to be also
a legal rule. In all legal systems the distinguishing characteristics of this stage are the feeling that
the legal must be made to coincide with the moral
at every point and the consequent progression of
moral ideas into legal ideas, and from what had
been but morals without legal sanction into effective legal institutions. The science of law begins
in this stage. Consequently as he looked back at
it the historical jurist could say that morals were
potential law. That which started as a moral
principle became an equitable principle and then

---

[56] E.g., see *Doctor and Student*, Dial. II, chap. 24 (1523);
Day v. Slaughter, Prec. Ch. 16 (1690); *Fursaker v. Robinson*,
Prec. Ch. 475 (1717); *Chapman v. Gibson*, 3 Bro. C. C. 229
(1791).

a rule of law.[57] What had seemed to the philosophical jurist of the law-of-nature school to show the identity of the moral and the legal, seemed to the historical jurist to show that they were distinct. But the historical jurist wrote from the standpoint of another stage of legal development.

It is not too much to say that the attempt to make law and morals identical by covering the whole field of morals with legal precepts, and by conforming existing precepts to the requirements of a reasoned system of morals, made the modern law. When the analytical jurist analyzes the precepts and doctrines and institutions of developed law and, in the apt language of Mr. Justice Holmes, washes the results "in cynical acid,"[58] and thus finds fundamental legal conceptions of right and duty and power and liberty or privilege devoid of any moral content, he much deceives himself. The legal right and legal duty of nineteenth-century law are but the natural right and moral duty of philosophical jurisprudence of the

---

[57] Compare: "Law and equity are in continual progression; and the former is constantly gaining ground upon the latter. Every new and extraordinary interposition is, by length of time, converted into an old rule. A great part of what is now strict law was formerly considered as equity; and the equitable decisions of this age will unavoidably be ranked under the strict law of the next." Millar, *Historical View of the English Government*, II, 358 (1812).

[58] *Collected Papers*, 174.

two preceding centuries taken over and given
more definite content in the maturity of law.
Jurists began by assuming that if they were moral,
and to the extent that they were moral, they were
therefore legal. Then the analytical jurist assuming that he could examine them as purely
legal institutions, reached his cynical conclusion
and justified it by deduction from his hypothesis.
Such phenomena as the doctrine that performance
of a moral obligation that cannot be coerced legally will stand legally as performance of a duty
and so is not a "voluntary" disposition of which
legal creditors may complain;[59] or that where a
moral duty is performed by mistake, although it
was not legally enforceable, the moral claim of
the recipient to hold what he has received will
stand as "consideration;"[60] or that a moral claim
to money may in effect be set off in equity against
a legal debt, although the claim is not directly enforceable at law, on the ground that the legal
creditor who seeks equity "must do equity"[61]—
such examples, and a score of others that might
be advanced, show that the legal system itself did
not wash the whole content of "right" and "duty"

[59] E.g., *Cottrell v. Snaith,* 63 Ia. 181; *Holden v. Barnes,* 140
Pa. St. 63; *Martin v. Remington,* 100 Wis. 540.

[60] *Farmer v. Arundel,* 2 W. Bl. 824.

[61] *Hemphill v. Moody,* 64 Ala. 468.

with cynical acid, whatever jurists may have tried
to do with the abstract conceptions. But in England at the end of the eighteenth century juristic
creative energy was spent. Lord Mansfield was
succeeded by Lord Kenyon. Lord Eldon came
presently to "crystallize" equity. A generation
later the creative energy that was needed for the
reception of the common law in America and
the reshapings and adaptations and assimilations
from the civil law, from the Continental commercial law, and from colonial custom, which that
process involved—that creative energy was spent
also. Instead of using "what ought to be" to
demonstrate "what is," jurists began to consider
"what is" to be an authentic pronouncement on
natural law. Much of the disrepute of natural
law at present comes from thinking of it in terms
of the identification of an ideal form of familiar
legal institutions with the postulated eternal immutable law of nature, which obtained at the end
of the eighteenth century, rather than in terms of
the classical creative natural law of the seventeenth century. Historical jurisprudence put a
historical foundation under the former way of
thinking.

Throughout the world the latter part of the
nineteenth century is a period of maturity of law.

The moral institutions and doctrines taken into the legal system during the period of growth become legalized. We get a "system" of equity. Equitable doctrines, such, for example, as equitable estoppel, acquire legal shells. The English Chancery Division tells us that it is "not a court of conscience."[62] The action for money had and received, which Lord Mansfield had made into a bill in equity at law, comes to be administered on mechanical principles.[63] More than one equitable conception is worked out into hard and fast rules which in their technical operations fall upon just and unjust alike. The administrative judicial methods of the seventeenth and eighteenth centuries give way to judicial methods which ignore results and seek abstract uniformity, formal predicability and outward appearance of certainty, at any cost. Thus a certain opposition between law and morals develops once more, and the historical jurist, writing with that phenomenon before his eyes, conceives that the very circumstance that this opposition has developed in the history of law demonstrates its validity, since it shows the course of realization of the idea.

---

[62] Buckley, J., in *In re Telescriptor Syndicate* [1903] 2 Ch. 174, 195-196.

[63] E.g., in *Baylis v. Bishop of London* [1913] 1 Ch. 127.

On such grounds the nineteenth-century jurist is zealous to point out that a legal right is not necessarily right—i.e., that it may or may not be accordant with general feelings as to what ought to be.[64] He is eager to show that one may have a legal claim that is morally wrong and to refute the fallacious jingle that a legal right is not a right if it is not right.[65] It may not be denied that the identification of morals and law, the assumption that propositions as to what ought to be might be asserted as authoritative legal precepts on that basis alone, gave rise to confusions that were injurious to clear thinking in the maturity of law. Yet the sharp line between making or finding the law and applying the law, which the

---

[64] "If it is a question of legal right, all depends upon the readiness of the State to exert its force on his behalf. It is hence obvious that a moral and a legal right are so far from being identical that they may easily be opposed to one another." Holland, *Jurisprudence* (12 ed.) 87. "Laws, as Austin has shown, must be legally binding and yet a law may be unjust. Resistance to authority cannot be a legal right, and yet it may be a virtue. But these are only examples. Into whatever discussions the words 'right' and 'justice' enter we are on the brink of a confusion from which a careful observance of the distinction between law and morals can alone save us. Austin has shown not only what law is but what it is not. He has determined accurately the boundaries of its province. The domain he assigns to it may be small, but it is indisputable. He has admitted that the law itself may be immoral, in which case it is our moral duty to disobey it; but it is nevertheless law." Markby, *Elements of Law* (4 ed.) § 12. See Gray, *Nature and Sources of the Law* (2 ed.) 14; Pollock, *Essays in Jurisprudence and Ethics*, 25-26 (1882).

[65] "An act contrary to right (*droit*) cannot give rise to a right (*droit*) even by the omnipotence of a law (*loi*)." Duguit, *Traité de droit constitutionnel*, (2 ed.) I, 157.

analytical jurist drew and the historical jurist accepted, cannot be maintained. Except for routine
cases, the analytical jurist grossly underestimated
the role of morals in everyday decision. Morals
do more than serve as a last resort when all· else
fails. If, as Gray asserts, moral ideas and statutory provisions are but raw materials from which
courts make the law by judicial decision,[66] using
the former when case-law and statute are want-
ing, the argument when carried out shows that the
judicial decisions of the past are but raw materials for the judicial decisions of the moment.
The outcome of the argument is that courts decide without law on the basis of sources of law.
It proves too much. If the term "law" is to have
any useful meaning it must include all the immediate materials of judicial decision.

Judges and lawyers felt this even at the height
of the reign of nineteenth-century theory. Thus
Judge Dillon, after stating the analytical and historical doctrine of the last century, to which from
a scientific juristic position he felt bound to as-
sent, could not but see that his experience as
counsel and as judge belied it. He says: "If un-
blamed I may advert to my own experience, I always felt in the exercise of the judicial office

---

[66] *Nature and Sources of the Law* (2 ed.) 84, 170.

irresistibly drawn to the intrinsic justice of the case, with the inclination, and if possible the determination, to rest the judgment upon the very right of the matter. In the practice of the profession I always feel an abiding confidence that if my case is morally right and just it will succeed, whatever technical difficulties may stand in the way; and the result usually justifies the confidence."[67] Theories that ignore such facts of the administration of justice are as much "in the air" as any philosophical theory ever was.

Sound thinking requires us to perceive that moral propositions do not become authoritatively established legal precepts whenever a jurist succeeds in demonstrating to his own satisfaction that they are ethically well taken. On the other hand, the conclusion of Historicus does not follow. He says: "It is right that a man should keep all his promises, but the law only compels him to keep those which are made for valuable consideration; yet the law is not therefore unjust; it only shows that the provinces of law and morality are not co-extensive."[68] They are not necessarily co-extensive. Many things are involved

---

[67] *Laws and Jurisprudence of England and America,* 17 (1894). See Fry, *Memoir of Sir Edward Fry,* 67.

[68] Letters by Historicus [Sir William Vernon Harcourt] on *Some Questions of International Law,* 76 (1863).

in determining how far the legal and the moral may be or should be made to coincide in a particular situation. But a legal rule can not stand simply on the basis that it is authoritatively established and is unmoral. The answer to Historicus is that for a generation the courts have been quietly loading his typical unmoral legal rule with exceptions and that judicial endeavor to attain justice through law is continually devising new means of evading it.[69] The circumstance that "a right" and "law" and abstract "right" in the ethical sense were all expressed in Latin by the same word, and that "a right" and abstract "right" in the ethical sense are expressed by the same word in English, has had a powerful influence in the history of law in bringing legal rights and legal rules into accord with right. It was a service to make us think out our terminology with more discrimination. But we must not take our logical discriminations for ends. Legal precepts sometimes are, and perhaps sometimes must be, at variance with the requirements of morals. Yet such a condition is not something of which the jurist is to be proud. It is not a virtue in the law to have it so. Nor are such conditions required, in a certain number, in order to demon-

---

[69] See Pound, *Introduction to the Philosophy of Law*, 271-273.

strate that law is one thing and morals another. So far as such things are more than historical anomalies that ought to be pruned away, they arise from inherent practical limitations upon effective legal action, which make it impossible or inexpedient in a wise social engineering to attempt to secure certain claims or enforce certain duties to the extent that might be desirable from a purely ethical standpoint.

II

THE ANALYTICAL VIEW

Analytical jurisprudence broke with philosophy and with ethics completely.[1] The historical school took over, from what may well be called metaphysical jurisprudence, the idealistic interpretation of legal history, and accepted the metaphysical juristic conception of the end of law and the metaphysical identification of the idea which was unfolding or realizing in legal history. The analytical jurists, on the other hand, regarded the

---

[1] "With the goodness or badness of laws as tried by the test of utility (or by any of the various tests which divide the opinions of mankind) it has no immediate concern." Austin, *Jurisprudence*, (3 ed.) 1107.

"The great gain in its fundamental conceptions which jurisprudence made during the last century was the recognition of the truth that the law of a state or other organized body is not an ideal, but something which actually exists. It is not that which is in accordance with religion, or nature, or morality; it is not that which ought to be, but that which is." Gray, *The Nature and Sources of the Law*, § 213 (1909), (2 ed.) 94.

"What, however, Austin's predecessors do not appear to me to have fully comprehended, at least not with that sure and firm grasp which proceeds from a full conviction, is the distinction between law and morals. We find, for example, that Bentham, when drawing the line between jurisprudence and ethics, classes legislation under jurisprudence, whereas, as Austin has shown, it clearly belongs to ethics. Austin, by establishing the distinction between law and morals . . . laid the foundation for a science of law." Markby, *Elements of Law* (4 ed.) § 12 (1889). The same proposition, stated with less assurance, may be found in the first edition (1871) 5-6.

See also Salmond's comments, *First Principles of Jurisprudence*, 36.

As to the relation of analytical jurisprudence to utilitarian ethics, see Maine, *Early History of Institutions* (American ed.) 308-309.

science of law as wholly self-sufficient.[2] Instead
of seeking to deduce a system from the nature of
man, or to deduce an ideal body of principles
from some assumed or metaphysically demonstrated first principle, they sought to take legal
precepts exactly as they were—as one of them put
it, to take the "pure fact of law"[3]—to analyze
actually existing legal institutions, and to obtain
in that way the materials for a universal science
of law. In practice they by no means succeeded
in confining themselves to "the pure fact of law."
It has been charged with much reason that both
analytical and historical jurists set up systems of
natural law of their own.[4] That is, each set up
ideal patterns to which all law should conform,
and by which all legal precepts were to be judged.
But it was not an ethical pattern, as it had been
during the vogue of natural law. The ideal pattern of the analytical jurist was one of a logically
consistent and logically interdependent system of

[2] Austin, *The Province of Jurisprudence Determined,* 1 (1832).
"It has been truly said that he who could perfectly classify the
law would have a perfect knowledge of the law." Gray, *Nature
and Sources of the Law,* § 15, (2 ed.) 3.

[3] Amos, *Systematic View of the Science of Jurisprudence,* 19
(1872).

[4] Brunner in Holtzendorff, *Enzyklopädie der Rechtswissenschaft* (5 ed.) 346-347; Kohler, *Rechtsphilosophie und Universalrechtsgeschichte,* in Holtzendorff *Enzyklopädie der Rechtswissenschaft* (6 ed.) I, 2.

legal precepts, completely covering the whole field of human relations, so far as they could become the subject of controversy, made at one stroke upon a logical plan to which it conformed in every detail. One need not say that this was quite as ideal and quite as far from "pure fact" as the older conception of a rational body of precepts, covering completely the field of morals and coinciding wholly with moral precepts in its details. Where the school of natural law had found the necessary *fundamenta* of law, the universal principles on which all law must rest, through philosophy, the analytical jurist sought to find them through analysis of the rules and doctrines and institutions of English law, of Roman law, and of the modern Roman law.[5]

Analytical jurisprudence assumed that "law" was an aggregate of rules of law, and took for the type of a rule of law, in the earlier stage of the school an English statute,[6] in the later stage an Anglo-American common-law rule of prop-

---

[5] "It is a general theory of law drawn almost entirely from Roman and English law." Bergbohm, *Jurisprudenz und Rechtsphilosophie,* 333 note (1892). "I mean, then, by general jurisprudence, the science concerned with the exposition of the principles, notions, and distinctions which are common to systems of law; understanding by systems of law, the ampler and maturer systems which, by reason of their amplitude and maturity, are preëminently pregnant with instruction." Austin, *Jurisprudence,* (3 ed.) II, 1108.

[6] E.g., see Bentham, *Principles of Morals and Legislation* 330-332.

erty or rule of commercial law.[7]   Hence it excluded from consideration much which, if not
"pure fact of law," was at least significant fact of
the legal order and controlling fact in the administration of justice. Also the analytical view of the
relation of law and morals was influenced strongly
by the dogma of separation of powers and consequent assumption that the making of legal precepts, on the one hand, and the interpretation and
application of them, on the other, could be kept
apart by an exact analytically drawn line and
could be committed exclusively to two distinct
organs of political society.[8]

Assuming an exact logically defined separation
of powers, the analytical jurist contended that

---

[7] Austin was a chancery barrister at a time when English
equity was chiefly taken up with the enforcement of family
settlements and trusts, and the equity lawyer was of necessity
an expert in the law of real property.   Hence he thought of
law largely in terms of the rules of the law of property.   This
attitude has colored Anglo-American analytical jurisprudence
ever since.   Professor Gray, our leading American writer from
the analytical standpoint, was above all a real property lawyer.
    Analytical definitions of law as an aggregate of rules, and of a
law as a rule, are significant.   Holland, *Jurisprudence* (12 ed.)
42; Markby, *Elements of Law*, § 7; Anson, *Law and Custom of
the Constitution*, I, 8; Gray, *The Nature and Sources of the
Law* (2 ed.) 95.
    As to the types of legal precept which this mode of thinking
ignores, see Pound, *The Administrative Application of Legal
Standards*, 44 Rep. Am. Bar Ass'n, 445, 454-458; *The Theory of
Judicial Decision*, 36 Harv. Law Rev. 641, 644-646; *Juristic
Science and Law*, 31 Harv. Law Rev. 1047, 1060-1062.
    [8] This is apparent beneath the surface in analytical jurispru-
dence even though the analytical jurists insist rightly that much
law is made by judicial decision.   See Austin, *Province of Jurisprudence Determined*, 28; Holland, *Jurisprudence*, (12 ed.) 78;
Markby, *Elements of Law*, (1 ed.) § 43.

law and morals were distinct and unrelated and
that he was concerned only with law.[9] If he saw
that their spheres came in contact or even over-
lapped in practice, he assumed that it was because
while in a theoretically fully developed legal system judicial and legislative functions are wholly
separated, this separation has not yet been realized to its full extent in practice. He would say:
So far as and where this separation is still incom-
plete there is still confusion of or overlapping between law and morals. From his standpoint
there were four such points of contact, namely,
in judicial lawmaking, in interpretation of legal
precepts, in the application of law, especially in
the application of legal standards, and in judicial
discretion. At these four points he conceived
there was a border line where the separation of
powers was not complete. So far as the separation of judicial and legislative powers was complete, law was for courts, morals were for legis-
lators; legal precepts were for jurisprudence,
moral principles were for ethics. But so far as
the separation was not yet complete and in what

---

[9] Austin, *Jurisprudence* (3 ed.) II, 1107; Gray, *Nature and
Sources of the Law* (1 ed.) §§ 1, 213, (2 ed.) 94, 139n. "The
science of jurisprudence deals with the facts brought to light
through the operation on the fact of law (considered as such,
and neither as good nor bad) of all other facts whatsoever."
Amos, *Systematic View of the Science of Jurisprudence,* 18
(1872).

the analytical jurist took to be the continually narrowing field in which judges must make as well as administer legal precepts, morality perforce must stand for the law which should but did not exist as the rule of judicial action.[10]

Thus two false assumptions are at the basis of the analytical doctrine. In the first place, the attempt to confine governmental action to an analytical scheme of threefold division of powers has simply failed. As actually drawn in American constitutional law today, the lines are more and more historical; and many commonwealths have expressly abrogated them in order to give powers of efficient action to their public service commissions. Everywhere experience of the impossibility of the thing has driven courts to recognize that sharp analytical lines cannot be drawn. Specialization of function for typical forms of governmental action, with a drawing of the lines on grounds of expediency in the large no man's land that surrounds each type, has proved the

---

[10] Thus, Austin argued for a codification which should be "a complete and exclusive body of statute law." *Jurisprudence* (3 ed.) II, 682. He held that the "incognoscibility" of "judiciary law" was due to the legislator's negligence. Id. 676. Until such a code, the judges, in the absence of legislation, "impress rules of positive morality with the character of law through decision of causes." Id. I, 37. See also Markby, *Elements of Law* (6 ed.) §§ 25-30.

As to the points of contact, see Austin, *Jurisprudence*, lect. 37, 38, and note on interpretation (3 ed.) II, 1023 ff.; Amos, *Science of Law*, 34-42.

most that could be achieved.[11]   Again, jurists
have had to give over the ideal of a complete
body of legal precepts which would require no
supplementing by judicial action.   It was an
eighteenth-century idea that a body of enacted
law might be made so complete and so perfect
that the judge would have only to select the exact
precept made in advance for the case in hand,

---

[11] *Federalist*, no. 47.   "The classification cannot be very exact
and there are many officers whose duties cannot properly, or at
least exclusively, be arranged under any of these heads."   Cooley,
Torts, 375.   "The assumption that governmental power is divis-
ible into mutually exclusive kinds of action has proved inappli-
cable to the concrete problems of government.   No classification
of powers, based upon the nature of the body to which any kind
of action is commonly delegated, can furnish mutually exclusive
kinds of power, capable of differentiation by reason of their intrinsic qualities."   Powell, *Separation of Powers*, 27 Political
Science Quarterly, 215, 237.   See 2 Willoughby, *Constitutional
Law of the United States*, §§ 742-743.

For judicial pronouncements, see *Murray* v. *Hoboken Land &
Improvement Co.*, 18 How. 274, 284; *Maynard v. Hill*, 125 U. S.
190, 204-209; *State v. Harmon*, 31 Ohio St. 250, 258.   In *Brown
v. Turner*, 70 N. C. 93, 102, Bynum, J., said: "While it is true
that 'the executive, legislative, and supreme judicial powers of
the government ought to be forever separate and distinct,' it is
also true that the science of government is a practical one;
therefore, while each should firmly maintain the essential powers
belonging to it, it cannot be forgotten that the three co-ordinate
parts constitute one brotherhood, whose common trust requires a
mutual toleration of the occupancy of what seems to be 'a common because of vicinage' bordering the domains of each."

For the separation of powers in practical application in recent
decision, compare Intermountain Rate Cases, 234 U. S. 476 with
the same case below, 191 Fed. 856.   Of this decision Taft, C. J.,
says: "The Interstate Commerce Commission was authorized to
exercise powers the conferring of which by Congress would have
been, perhaps, thought in the earlier years of the Republic to
violate the rule that no legislative power can be delegated.   But
the inevitable progress and exigencies of government and the
utter inability of Congress to give the time and attention indispensable to the exercise of these powers in detail, forced the
modification of the rule."   257 U. S., xxv-xxvi.

and then mechanically apply it.[12] Such an idea
is to be seen occasionally today, when some poli-
tician urges a measure of legislation which shall
define everything exactly *a priori,* and leave nothing to judges and lawyers beyond ascertainment
of the facts and a logical cramming of them into
the pre-appointed statutory pigeonholes. But this
ideal also has failed us in practice. Today, so
far as any jurist believes in the possibility of a
complete system leaving nothing to judicial making as distinguished from judicial finding, he expects to realize it only through a complete logical
system of fundamental analytical propositions or
historical principles, in which the solution of
every particular controversy is logically implicit
and from which a rule of decision for every case
may be deduced by a mechanical logical process.[13]

Granting, however, that the two assumptions
on which the analytical divorce of jurisprudence
from ethics proceeds are not maintainable, we do
not dispose entirely of the contention of the analytical school. For although we admit that legislator and judge each make and shape and develop

---

[12] E.g., see the preface to the *Code of Frederick the Great,* §
28 (English transl. *The Frederician Code,* I. pp. xxxviii-xl).
Compare Sir Samuel Romilly on *Bentham's Writings on Codification,* 29 Edinburgh Review, 224.

[13] This proposition is often stated in terms of a metaphysical
natural law. E.g., Bishop, *Non-Contract Law,* §§ 84-88.

and extend or restrict legal precepts, there is a difference of the first moment between legislative lawmaking and judicial lawmaking. The legislative lawmaker is laying down a rule for the future.[14] Hence the general security does not require him to proceed on predetermined premises or along predetermined lines. He may take his premises from whencesoever his wisdom dictates and proceed along the lines that seem best to him. On the other hand, the judicial lawmaker is not merely making a rule for the future. He is laying down a legal precept which will apply to the transactions of the past as well as to the future and he is doing so immediately with reference to a controversy arising in the past.[15] Hence the social interest in the general security requires that

[14] He may, unless constitutions forbid, law down rules by which the past is to be judged. But such legislation is universally reprobated and has been forbidden in formulations of fundamental law from the Twelve Tables to modern constitutions. The French Civil Code, art. 2, provides: "The enacted rule only makes dispositions for the future; it has no retroactive effect." Baudry-Lacantinerie says of this: "In a well organized society individuals ought not to be exposed to having their condition or fortune compromised by a change of legislation. There must be some security in transactions; but there is none if laws may operate retroactively, for the right I have acquired today in conformity to the provisions of the existing law may be taken from me tomorrow by a law which I could not have taken into account since it was impossible to foresee it." *Précis de droit civil* (11 ed.) I, § 45. See XII Tab. ix, 1 (Bruns, *Fontes Iuris Romani Antiqui* (6 ed.) I, 34); Clark, *Australian Constitutional Law*, 28 ff.; Const. Brazil, arts. 15, 791; Dodd, *Modern Constitutions*, I, 153, 176.

[15] "It must be observed that a judicial decision *primae impressionis*, or a judgment by which a new point of law is for the first time decided, is always an *ex post facto* law." Austin, *Jurisprudence* (3 ed.) I, 503.

he should not have the same freedom as the legislative lawmaker. It requires that instead of finding his premises or his materials of decision where he will or where expediency appears to him to dictate, he find them in the legal system or by a process recognized by the legal system. It requires that instead of proceeding along the lines that seem best to him, he proceed along lines which the legal system prescribes or at least recognizes.

Thus the proposition that a judicial decision is only evidence of the law, the doctrine that judges always find the law and never make it, are not without an important purpose.[16] If they are dogmatic fictions, they do more than enable us to arrange the phenomena of the administration of

---

[16] "Story, J., probably knew as well as John Austin that judges make law. But he probably knew better than John Austin the legal and constitutional restraints imposed on judges in the United States when engaged in the process of making law. The legislative process of making law and the judicial process of making law are, of course, widely different. Both are subject to like constitutional and legal restraints, but there are other and different constitutional and legal restraints peculiar to the judicial process, and especially peculiar to it in the United States. No judge in England or in the United States ever did need to be told, I think, that he has power to make law, but many judges in England and in the United States have needed to be reminded from time to time, vi et armis, of the constitutional and legal restraints binding upon them, when engaged in the judicial process of making law; and few, indeed, have been the judges, especially in the United States, who have shown a sound understanding as to when those restraints are rigid, and when they are elastic and flexible. When you say judges only declare pre-existing law, and do not make new law, you emphasize those restraints and keep them fresh in the memory better than when you say judges make law." Schofield, *Essays on Constitutional Law and Equity*, I, 42-43.

justice in a convenient, logically consistent scheme. They grow out of a sound instinct of judges and lawyers for maintaining a paramount social interest. They serve to safeguard the social interest in the general security by requiring the grounds of judicial decision to be as definite as is compatible with the attainment of justice in results. They serve to make judicial action predicable so far as may be. They serve to hold down the personality of the magistrate. They serve to constrain him to look at causes objectively and try them by reasoned development of legal materials which had taken shape prior to and independent of the cause in hand. Hence where rules are laid down for the future only, the lawmaker is given entire freedom, subject in America to a few reservations in bills of rights. Where, as in judicial lawmaking, rules are laid down for past as well as for future situations, the lawmaker is held down to traditional premises or traditional legal materials and to traditional lines and modes of development, to the end that those who know the tradition may be able within reasonable limits to forecast his action.

Ideals are required not merely for legislative but quite as much for judicial making or finding or shaping of legal precepts and for judicial application of legal precepts. Yet the reviving natural law of today must recognize the limitations imposed upon judicial creative activity, and must not seek to make the judge as free to pursue his own ideals in his own way as is the legislator. This can not be urged too strongly upon lay critics of the courts. They overlook as a rule the important difference between the process of legislative lawmaking and the process of incidental selection of legal materials and giving them shape as legal precepts, which is involved in not a little of judicial decision. The latter may be called judicial lawmaking without any reflection upon the courts. The social interest in the general security requires us to maintain such a distinction.

A second point of contact between law and morals is to be found in interpretation.[17] Interpretation has been thought of as including the process of finding or making rules for new cases, or reshaping them for unusual cases, which has just been considered. That form of so-called interpretation, so called by a dogmatic fiction, because in analytical theory the law is complete and all cases are at least covered by the logical implica-

---

[17] 1 Blackstone, *Commentaries*, 85-91; Austin, *Jurisprudence* (3 ed.) 1023-1036; Clark, *Practical Jurisprudence*, 230-244; Pound, *Spurious Interpretation*, 7 Columbia Law Rev. 379; Gray, *Nature and Sources of the Law*, §§ 370-399, 2 ed. 170-189; Geny, *Méthode d'interprétation* (2 ed.) I, §§ 92-108, II, §§ 177-187; Stammler, *Theorie der Rechtswissenschaft*, 558-652; Heck, *Gesetzesauslegung und Interessenjurisprudenz*, §§ 1-16; W. Jellinek, *Gesetz, Gesetzesanwendung und Zweckmässigkeitserwägung.*

tions of pre-existing rules or the logical content of legal principles, was set off by Austin under the name of "spurious interpretation."[18] Here the contact between law and morals is obvious, since the process is within limits one of legislation. But in what Austin called "genuine interpretation," the search for the actual meaning of those who prescribed a rule admittedly governing the case in hand, the final criterion, when literal meaning and context fail to yield a satisfactory construction, is found in the "intrinsic merit" of the various possible meanings.[19] The judge or jurist assumes that the lawmaker intended to prescribe a just rule. He assumes that the lawmaker's ideas as to what is just and his own ideas thereof are in substantial accord; he assumes that each holds substantially to the same ideal pattern of law or ideal picture of society and of the end of law as determined thereby. However much the analytical theory of "genuine interpretation" may purport to exclude the moral ideas of the judge, and to insure a wholly mechanical logical

---

[18] *Jurisprudence* (3 ed.) 596-597, 650-651, 1025-1030; Clark, *Practical Jurisprudence*, 235-242; Clark, *Roman Private Law: Jurisprudence*, I, 114-125.

[19] Savigny, *System des heutigen römischen Rechts*, I, §§ 34, 37; Clark, *Practical Jurisprudence*, 234-235. Among the five means of genuine interpretation in French law, the fourth is "to weigh the consequences which the legal precept would produce according to whether one understood it in the one sense or in the other." Baudry-Lacantinerie, *Précis de droit civil*, I, § 100.

exposition of a logically implied content of legal precepts, two doors are left open. The court must determine whether the criteria of the literal meaning of the words and of the text read with the context yield a "satisfactory" solution. If he holds that they do not, he must inquire into the "intrinsic merit" of the competing interpretations. "Satisfactory" will almost always mean in practice, morally satisfactory. "Intrinsic merit" will always tend to mean intrinsic ethical merit.[20]

---

[20] "I think it difficult to express the amount of importance involved in this decision. The principle of it comprises such a state of things as this: A man builds a house upon his own land, and he builds it to a certain extent forwards, that is, towards the roadway of a street. It may be that in truth and in fact, and as everybody afterwards would be of opinion upon seeing the place, he has not built it beyond the real line of buildings of the street, that, in truth and in fact, he has merely used his own property and has not contravened that which is the real object of the statute; and it may be that the architect, as has been suggested in former cases, either has taken somewhat too strictly a mathematical view of the matter, or has made a mistake. It may be that he himself would be ready to acknowledge that he has made a mistake. And yet it is contended that the magistrate, by this legislation, is bound to order a person who has built his own house, at his on cost, on his own land, to pull it down, and that the first legal tribunal before which the case comes, is bound to make an order and to do a great injustice. It may be that that is the law. If that is the true interpretation of the statute, if there are no means of avoiding such an interpretation of the statute, a judge must come to the conclusion that the legislature by inadvertence has committed an act of legislative injustice; but to my mind a judge ought to struggle with all the intellect that he has, and with all the vigour of mind that he has, against such an interpretation of an Act of Parliament." Brett, M. R., in *Plumstead Board of Works v. Spackman*, 13 Q. B. D. 878, 886-887.

"If a statute be susceptible of two constructions, one consistent with natural equity and justice and one inconsistent therewith, the court should give it that construction which comports with natural equity and justice." Blanford, J., in *Lombard v. Trustees*, 73 Ga. 322, 324.

LAW AND MORALS   57

"We are not satisfied with the reasoning of those cases and have been unable to reach the conclusion that a mere prospective legal heir, or devisee in a will, can make certain that which was uncertain, by his own felonious act, in the cold-blooded murder of the party from whom he or she expects to inherit. We do not believe that these courts have fully applied and used the canons of statutory construction which we have the right to use and ought to use to avoid a result so repugnant to common right and common decency. The construction as has been given such statutes bruises and wounds the finer sensibilities of every man. In the case at bar, the murdered woman, younger in years, might have outlived the prospective heir. The property involved in this very suit might have been used by her for her own comforts even though she had died first. Being hers it might have been sold and the proceeds disposed of by gift or otherwise. Can it be said that one, by high-handed murder, can not only make himself an heir in fact, when he had but a mere expectancy before, but further shall enjoy the fruits of his own crime? To us this seems abhorrent to all reason, and reason is the better element of the law." Graves, J., in *Perry v. Strawbridge,* 209 Missouri 621, 628-629.

In *Griffin v. Interurban St. Ry. Co.,* 179 N. Y. 438, a penal statute provided: "For every refusal to comply with the requirements of this section the corporation so refusing shall forfeit fifty dollars to the aggrieved party." In a series of prior decisions the New York Court of Appeals had held that where the words "each offence" or "every offence" were used cumulatively penalties had been provided for. In rendering the opinion of the court Bartlett, J., said: "There have been presented at the bar of this court, civil and criminal cases where the aggregate penalties sought to be recovered have amounted to enormous and well-nigh appalling sums by reason of plaintiffs permitting a long period to elapse before beginning actions. Actions of this nature have become highly speculative and present a phase of litigation that ought not to be encouraged."

"The court is of opinion that if cumulative recoveries are to be permitted, the legislature should state its intention in so many words; that a more definite form of statement be substituted for the words hitherto deemed sufficient." (p. 449)

"It is not just that a man should by virtue of this act be assessed to the payment of money, in the raising of which he could have no agency, or from which he could not (without any fault of his own) derive any benefit. Thus if he was included within a district, after the vote to raise the money had passed, it is admitted that he could not be assessed to the payment of it; for not being a member of the district when the money was voted, he could have had no voice in the vote. As he may by the act of his town, against his consent, be excluded from the district, by which the vote was passed, and included in another before the assessment is made, so he can derive no benefit from the payment of the assessment, and it is therefore unreasonable that he should be assessed. If by the alteration of the district a number of persons may be excluded, lessening the numbers, and wealth of the district, it would not be reasonable to assess the

Another point of contact is in the application of law.[21] Analytical jurists have liked to think of the application of legal precepts as a purely mechanical process. Such things as the margin of discretion in the application of equitable remedies, the appeal to the ethical in the maxims of equity, and the ethical element in such equitable doctrines as those with respect to "hard bargains," mistake coupled with "sharp practice," and the like, were distasteful to them. Partly under their influence and partly from the same spirit of the maturity of law that led to the analytical way of thinking, in the last quarter of the

whole sum on the remaining members, although they alone will have the benefit of it: for they might have refused to pass the vote to raise so large a sum of money. . . The true and necessary construction of the statute therefore requires that the district voting to raise the money should have the same limits when the money is assessed." Parsons, C. J., in *Richards v. Dagget,* 4 Mass. 534, 537.

See also *Ham v. McClaws,* 1 Bay (S. C.) 93, 96.

In the case first quoted, however, a majority of the Court of Appeal gave to the statute the construction which Brett, M. R., considered so unjust that some way of avoiding it must be found. Compare the majority opinion and the dissenting opinion of Lord Gordon in *River Wear Commissioners v. Adamson,* 2 A. C. 743, and see *Flint River Co. v. Foster,* 2 Ga. 194, 201-202.

See also the remarks of Lord Watson as to the "intention of the legislature," *Salmon v. Salmon & Co.,* [1897] A. C. 22, 38.

[21] *Science of Legal Method* (Modern Legal Philosophy Series, vol. 9) chaps. 1-5; Wigmore, *Problems of Law,* 65-101; Pound, *The Enforcement of Law,* 20 Green Bag, 401; Pound, *Courts and Legislation,* 7 American Political Science Review, 361-383 (also in *Science of Legal Method,* 202-228); Geny, *Méthode d'interprétation* (2 ed.) II, §§ 196-200; Brütt, *Die Kunst der Rechtsanwendung;* W. Jellinek, *Gesetz, Gesetzesanwendung und Zweckmässigkeitserwägung;* Somlo, *Juristische Grundlehre,* §§ 110-122; Heck, *Gesetzesauslegung und Interessenjurisprudenz,* § 2; Stampe, *Grundlegung der Wertbewegungslehre;* Ransson, *Essai sur l'art de juger.*

nineteenth century some American courts sought
to eliminate, or at least to minimize, the scope of
these doctrines, and to make equitable relief, once
jurisdiction was established, as much a matter of
course as damages at law.[22]   But this equitable
or individualized application of legal precepts is
called for more and more in the law of today.   It
is the life of administration, whether executive or
judicial.   The lack of power of individualization
in judicial decision in the immediate past has led
to a multiplication of executive administrative
commissions and administrative tribunals and a
transfer thereto of matters formerly of judicial
cognizance, which can but bring home to lawyers
the futility of nineteenth-century attempts to
make courts into judicial slot machines.[23]

In fact the ethical element in application of law
was never excluded from the actual administration of justice.   Our analytical science of law in
the last century did no more than cover up the

---

[22] E.g., see 4 Pomeroy, *Equity Jurisprudence,* § 1404 and note
2.   Compare the arbitrary rule as to mutuality of equitable relief
which developed in nineteenth-century American decisions with
the remarks of Cardozo, J., in *Epstein v. Gluckin,* 233 N. Y.
490, 494.

[23] "The growth in this country, during the past forty years, of
administrative regulation has been unparalleled and its expansion
and enveloping tendency are certain to continue." Address of
W. D. Guthrie, Esq., as President of the New York State Bar
Association, January 19, 1923.   See Pound, *Justice According to
Law—Executive Justice,* 14 Columbia Law Rev. 12; Pound, *The
Revival of Personal Government,* Proc. New Hampshire Bar
Ass'n, 1917, 13.   As to Europe, see Laun, *Das freie Ermessen
und seine Grenzen* (1910) with full bibliography.

actual process with dogmatic fictions that for a time made us blind to what we were doing and led to some unhappy attempts to reduce to rule things that do not admit of rule. It will suffice to note two aspects of application of law in which the ethical element has always been decisive—the application of legal standards, and judicial exercise of discretion. A great and increasing part of the administration of justice is achieved through legal standards. These standards come into the law, in the stage of infusion of morals, through theories of natural law.[24] They have to do with conduct, or with conduct of enterprises, and contain a large moral element. Thus the standard of due care in our law of negligence, the standard of fair competition, the standard of fair conduct of a fiduciary, the Roman standard of what good faith demands in a particular transaction, or the Roman standard of how a prudent and diligent person *sui juris* would act under such circumstances, all involve an idea of fairness or reasonableness. Furthermore like all moral precepts these legal standards are individualized in their application. They are not applied mechanically to a set of facts looked at in the abstract.

---

[24] Their origin is to be found in the formula in actions *bonae fidei—quicquid paret ob eam rem Numerium Negidium Aulo Agerio ex fide bona dare facere opportere.* See *Gaius,* iv, § 47; *Inst.* iv, 6, §§ 28, 30; Cicero, *De officiis,* iii, 17, 70.

They are applied according to the circumstances of each case, and within wide limits are applied through an intuition of what is just and fair, involving a moral judgment upon the particular item of conduct in question.[25]

---

[25] "Negligence is the failure to observe for the protection of the interests of another person that degree of care, precaution and vigilance which the circumstances justly demand, whereby such person suffers injury." Cooley, *Torts*, 630.

"Negligence is the omission to do something which a reasonable man, guided upon those considerations which ordinarily regulate the conduct of human affairs, would do, or doing something which a prudent and reasonable man would not do." Alderson, B., in *Blyth v. Birmingham Waterworks Co.*, 11 Ex. 781, 784.

That application of the standard of due care involves a moral judgment but is not a purely moral judgment, see Holmes, *The Common Law*, 107 ff.

"All charges made for any service rendered or to be rendered in the transportation of passengers or property and for the transmission of messages by telegraph, telephone, or cable, as aforesaid, or in connection therewith, shall be just and reasonable; and every unjust and unreasonable charge for such service or any part thereof is prohibited and declared to be unlawful. . .

"And it is hereby made the duty of all common carriers subject to the provisions of this act to establish, observe and enforce just and reasonable classifications . . . and just and reasonable regulations and practices . . . and every . . . unjust and unreasonable classification, regulation, and practice with reference to commerce between the states or with foreign countries is prohibited and declared to be unlawful." *Act to Regulate Commerce*, § 1.

As to application of these standards, see Pound, *Administrative Application of Legal Standards*, 44 Rep. Am. Bar Assn., 445, 456.

"Unfair methods of competition in commerce are hereby declared unlawful." *Federal Trade Commission Act*, § 5.

"[In case of transactions between attorney and client] on the one hand it is not necessary to establish that there has been fraud or imposition upon the client; and on the other hand it is not necessarily void throughout, *ipso facto*. But the burthen of establishing its perfect fairness, adequacy, and equity is thrown upon the attorney, upon the general rule that he who bargains in a matter of advantage with a person placing a confidence in him is bound to show that a reasonable use has been made of that confidence; a rule applying equally to all persons standing in confidential relations with each other." 1 Story, *Equity Jurisprudence*, § 311.

No less clearly there is a point of contact between law and morals in those matters which are
left to the personal discretion of the judge.   In
cases where there is a margin of discretion in the
application of legal precepts, as in the doctrines
of equity above referred to, we speak of "judicial" discretion.   Here there are principles governing judicial action within the discretionary margin of application, although at bottom there is not
a little room for personal moral judgment.   There
are many situations, however, where the course
of judicial action is left to be determined wholly
by the judge's individual sense of what is right
and just.[26]   Thus in imposition of sentences,
within certain legally fixed limits; in suspension
of sentence, where it is allowed; in the summary
jurisdiction of courts to prevent abuse of procedural rules; in the tribunals which are now setting up so generally for petty causes; in award-
ing the custody of children in some jurisdictions;
in the choice of trustees or guardians or receivers

In Roman law in actions arising out of guardianship, partnership, fiduciary pledge, mandate, sale, letting and hiring, to which
others were added later, "the judge had a larger discretion, and
the standard set before him was what was fairly to be expected
from businesslike men dealing with one another in good faith."
Roby, *Roman Private Law*, II, 89.   See Cicero, *De officiis*, iii,
17, 70; Cicero, *De natura deorum*, iii, 30, § 74; *Gaius*, iv, § 62;
Institutes, iv, 6, § 30.

[26] See Isaacs, *The Limits of Judicial Discretion*, 32 Yale Law
Journal, 339.

—in these and like cases judicial action must proceed largely on personal feelings as to what is right. , The objections to this element in the judicial function are obvious. It has been said that at best it is the "law of tyrants."[27] But hard as we tried in the last century to reduce it to the point of extinction, there has proved to be a point beyond which rule and mechanical application are impotent, and the tendency of the day is to extend rather than to restrict its scope. Perhaps the true way to make it tolerable is to recognize that here we are in the domain of ethics, and that ethics, too, is a science and not without principles.

It will have been noted that the analytical account of the points of contact between law and morals puts the matter as if there were three or four restricted areas in which exceptionally such contact may take place. Occasionally it may happen that a case arises for which there is no applicable legal precept and the judge must work one out for the case from the legal materials at hand, with the guidance of a certain traditional technique of analogical development of the precedents.[28] Occasionally, too, it may happen that an authoritatively established legal precept is so

---

[27] Lord Camden, quoted by Fearne, *Contingent Remainders,* (10 ed.) 534 note t. It need not be said that the law of property is not a suitable field for discretion.

[28] Austin, *Jurisprudence,* (3 ed.) II, 660-663.

ill-expressed that genuine interpretation becomes necessary. In that process it may happen that as a last resort the judge must pass upon the relative merit of the several possible interpretations from an ethical standpoint. Also, in those exceptional cases for which ordinary legal remedies are not adequate, a court of equity may have a certain margin of power to go upon the moral aspects of the case in granting or denying extraordinary relief. In a few matters there are "mixed questions of law and fact" where the trier of fact, in adjusting a legal standard to the facts of a particular case, may find opportunity for an incidental moral judgment. Finally a few matters of administration must be left to the magistrate's personal sense of right. All this looks as if in its everyday course judicial justice was quite divorced from ideas of right and moral justice, with intrusion of morals into the legal domain only in a residuum of cases for which adequate legal provision had not yet been made, or in which an administrative element still lingered in the courts instead of being committed to the executive. But this plausible explanation represents juristic desire for a certain, uniform, predicable justice much better than it represents judicial justice in action. In our appellate tribunals the difficulty that brings the cause up for review is usually that legal rules and legal conceptions have to be applied by analogy to causes that depart from the type for which the precept was devised or given shape. Such departures vary infinitely. Cases are seldom exactly alike. Hence choice from among competing analogies and choice from among competing modes of analogical development are the staple of judicial opinions.[29] The line between "genuine" and "spurious" interpretation can be drawn only for typical cases. They shade into one another and a wide zone between them is the field in which a great

---

[29] E.g., if one had to name six significant cases in the law of torts, I suspect they would be: *Pasley v. Freeman*, 3 T. R. 51 (1789); *Davies v. Mann*, 10 M. & W. 546 (1842); *Brown v. Kendall*, 6 Cush. 292 (1850); *Lumley v. Gye*, 2 E. & B. 216 (1853); *Rylands v. Fletcher*, L. R. 3 H. L. 330 (1868); *Heaven v. Pender* (opinion of Brett, J.) 11 Q. B. D. 503 (1883). But note how each one of them involves a choice between two possible lines of analogical reasoning and sets the law on some point in a path leading from some one analogy rather than from another. Thus in *Pasley v. Freeman* as between an analogy of warranty or of relation and one of assault—as between a contractual or relational and a delictual analogy—the court chose the latter and established a liability for intentional deceit although the defendant had in no wise profited by the deceit and although he was under no contract duty and was party to no relation which called on him to speak. Thus we get a principle of liability for aggression of one person upon another. *Lumley v. Gye* chose the analogy of injury to tangible property and so, we say, applied the same principle to intentional interference with advantageous relations. *Brown v. Kendall* is an epoch-making case choosing decisively between substantive conceptions on the one hand and procedural distinctions on the other hand, as the basis of liability for injuries due to culpable carrying out of a course of conduct not involving aggression. In *Heaven v. Pender* we get a thoroughgoing rational exposition of the resulting principle. *Rylands v. Fletcher* involved choice between the analogy of liability for culpable conduct and the analogy of liability (regardless of culpability) for the escape of animals and resulting damages. *Davies v. Mann* involved a choice between a procedural analogy of a bar to recovery and a substantive analogy of liability for culpably caused injury.

part of appellate decision must take place.[30] Likewise the extraordinary relief given by courts of equity has become the everyday form of justice for large classes of controversies and legislation has been adding new classes.[31] The transition to an urban, industrial society, which, as the last census shows, has definitely taken place for the country as a whole, calls for more summary, administrative, offhand justice, of the type formerly peculiar to petty courts, and tribunals with flexible procedure and wide powers of discretionary action are springing up everywhere. In truth, there are continual points of contact with morals at every turn in the ordinary course of judicial administration. A theory that ignores them, or pictures them as few and of little significance, is not a theory of the actual law in action.

Morals are more than potential materials for the legislative lawmaker. Ethics can serve us more than as a critique of proposed measures of

---

[30] This was recognized judicially long ago: "And the judges themselves do play the chancellor's part upon statutes, making construction of them according to equity, varying from the rules and grounds of law, and enlarging them *pro bono publico,* against the letter and intent of the makers, whereof our books have many hundreds of cases." Lord Ellesmere in *Earl of Oxford's Case,* 1 *White v. Tudor, Leading Cases in Equity,* (8 ed.) 773, 779.

[31] *Littleton v. Fritz,* 65 Ia. 488; *State v. Gilbert,* 126 Minn. 95; U. S. Act of July 2, 1890, § 4, 26 St. L. 209; N. Y. Penal Law, § 1217, Act of April 4, 1921, L. 1921 ch. 155.

lawmaking as they are presented to the legislator.
To that extent the analytical jurist was wrong.
But in another respect, and to a certain extent, he
was right. When we have found a moral principle we cannot stop at that. We have more to
do than to formulate it in a legal rule. We must
ask how far it has to do with things that may be
governed by legal rules. We must ask how far
legal machinery of rule and remedy are adapted
to the claims which it recognizes and would secure. We must ask how far, if we formulate a
precept in terms of our moral principle, it may be
made effective in action.[32] Even more we must
consider how far it is possible to give the moral
principle legal recognition and legal efficacy by
judicial action or juristic reasoning, on the basis
of the received legal materials and with the received legal technique, without impairing the
general security by unsettling the legal system as
a whole.[33] As the fifteenth-century lawyer said
in the Year Books, some things are for.the law of
the land, and some things are for the chancellor,
and some things are between a man and his
confessor.[34]

---

[32] See Pound, *The Limits of Effective Legal Action,* 3 Journ.
Am. Bar Assn., 55, 27 Int. Journ. Ethics, 150.

[33] 36 Harv. Law Rev. 947-948.

[34] Fineux, *arguendo* in *Anonymous,* Y. B. Hil. 4 Hen. 7, pl.
8, fol. 5.

What is it that sets off the domain of law and that of morals, assuming that their provinces are neither identical nor wholly distinct? If there are two forms or modes of social control, each covering much of the same ground, yet each having ground that is peculiarly its own, what determines the boundary between them? Is it a distinction in subject matter or in application of legal precepts, on the one hand, and moral principles, on the other, or is it both? Analytical jurists have assured us that it is both. In the last century they insisted much on the distinction in respect of subject matter, and on the distinction in respect of application. Let us see how they made these distinctions and how far their points are holding good in the stage of legal development upon which we are entering.

With respect to subject matter, it is said that morals have to do with thought and feeling, while the law has to do only with acts; that in ethics we aim at perfecting the individual character of men while law seeks only to regulate the relations of individuals with each other and with the state. It is said that morals look to what is behind acts, rather than to acts as such. Law, on the other hand, looks to acts, and only to thoughts and feelings so far as they indicate the character of acts and thus determine the danger to the general

security or the general morals which they involve.[35] The act with malice or *dolus* is more
anti-social than the one with mere stupidity or a
slow reaction time behind it. Hence, for example, the criminal law calls for a guilty mind.
But in a crowded community where mechanical
agencies of danger to the general security are in
everyday use, and many sorts of business activity
incidentally involve potential injury to society,
thoughtlessness and want of care, or stupidity, or
even neglect to supervise one's agent at his peril,
may be as anti-social as a guilty mind, and so a
group of legal offences may develop that take no
account of intent.[36]

---

[35] "For though *in foro conscientiae* a fixed design or will to do
an unlawful act is almost as heinous as the commission of it, yet
as no temporal tribunal can search the heart or fathom the in-
tentions of the mind, otherwise than as they are demonstrated
by outward actions, it cannot therefore punish for what it cannot
know." 4 Blackstone, *Commentaries*, 21.

"Now the state, that complains in criminal causes, does not
suffer from the mere imaginings of men. To entitle it to complain, therefore, some act must have followed the unlawful
thought. This doctrine is fundamental and in a general way
universal." 1 Bishop, *New Criminal Law*, § 204.

"The object of the law is not to punish sins, but is to prevent
certain external results." Holmes, J., in *Commonwealth v. Ken-
nedy*, 170 Mass. 18, 20.

See Amos, *Science of Law*, 32; Stone, *Law and Its Administration*, 33-35; Tissot, *Introduction philosophique à l'étude du
droit*, II, 252-255.

[36] "Public policy may require that in the prohibition or punishment of particular acts it may be provided that he who shall do
them shall do them at his peril and will not be heard to plead in
his defense good faith or ignorance." *Shevlin-Carpenter Co. v.
Minnesota*, 218 U. S. 57, 70. Compare *State v. Quinn*, 131 La.
490, 495; *Wells Fargo Express v. State*, 79 Ark. 349, 352 (statute
against shipment of game in interstate commerce—no defense

As to the other proposition, it is said that as between external and internal morality the law has to do with the former only. Thou shalt not covet thy neighbor's house is a moral rule. But unless covetousness takes outward form, e.g., in larceny, the law does not and indeed cannot deal with it.[37] Not that the law closes its eyes to the internal. But law operates through sanctions— through punishment, substitutional redress, specific redress, or forcible prevention. Hence it must have something tangible upon which to go. The story of the schoolmaster who said, "Boys be pure in heart or I'll flog you," is in point.[38] Purity in speech and act is the most that the penalty of flogging can insure. Because of the practical limitations involved in application and administration, this point made by the analytical jurist is well taken. The lawmaker must remember these practical limitations and must not suppose that he can bring about an ideal social order

---

that carrier did not know contents of parcel shipped); *Welch v. State*, 145 Wis. 86 (statute as to sale of oleomargarine—no defense that substance served was sent to defendant in response to an order for butter and *bona fide* believed by him to be butter); *State v. Laundy*, 103 Or. 443 ("criminal syndicalism" act—no matter whether or not accused who joined I. W. W. knew the nature and purposes of the organization); *Hobbs v. Winchester Corporation* [1910] 2 K. B. 471.

[37] Pollock, *First Book of Jurisprudence*, (4 ed.) 46-47.
[38] Id. 47, note 1.

by law if only he can hit upon the proper moral principles and develop them properly by legislation.

But nineteenth-century jurists were inclined to carry this argument too far and to ignore moral considerations merely as such—to ignore those which the law can and should take into account, and to assume that they might do so simply on the ground of the distinction between the legal and the moral. Because it is impracticable to make the moral duty of gratitude into a legal duty, it does not follow that the law is to deal only with affirmative action and not seek to enforce tangible moral duties not involving affirmative action even though legal enforcement is practicable.

For example, take the case of damage to one which is clearly attributable to wilful and morally inexcusable inaction of another. Suppose a case where there is no relation between the two except that they are both human beings. If the one is drowning and the other who is at hand and has a rope is inert, if he sits on the bank and smokes when he could act without the least danger, the law has refused to impose liability. As Ames puts it : "He took away nothing from a person in jeopardy, he simply failed to confer a benefit upon a stranger. . . . The law does not compel

active benevolence between man and man. It is
left to one's conscience whether he will be the
good Samaritan or not."[39]

What difficulties are there here to make the law
hesitate? To some extent there are difficulties of
proof. We must be sure the one we hold culpable was not dazed by the emergency.[40] Again, he
who fails to act may assert some claim that must
be weighed against the claim of him whom he
failed to help. Thus, in the good Samaritan case
the priest and the Levite may have had good
cause to fear robbers, if they tarried on the way
and were not at the inn before sunset. Also, it
may sometimes be difficult to say upon whom the
legal duty of being the good Samaritan shall de-
volve. If John Doe is helpless and starving, shall
he sue Henry Ford or John D. Rockefeller? But
the case of an athletic young man with a rope and
life belt at hand, who sits on a bench in a park
along a river bank and sees a child drown, does
not present these difficulties. Yet the law makes
no distinction. Practical difficulties are not always or necessarily in the way. In the case put
there is nothing intrinsic in the moral principle

---

[39] Ames, *Law and Morals*, 22 Harvard Law Rev. 97, 112. See
also Bohlen, *The Moral Duty to Aid Others as a Basis of Tort
Liability*, 56 University of Pennsylvania Law Rev. 217, 316;
Bruce, *Humanity and the Law*, 73 Central Law Journ. 335.

[40] See Rivers, *Instinct and the Unconscious*, 55.

which should prevent legal recognition of it and
the working out of appropriate legal rules to give
it effect. Indeed a movement in this direction is
visible in recent American decisions.[41] We must
reject the opposition of law and morals when
pushed so far as to justify ignoring the moral
aspects of such a case as this.

As to application of moral principles and legal
precepts respectively, it is said that moral principles are of individual and relative application;
they must be applied with reference to circumstances and individuals, whereas legal rules are
of general and absolute application. Hence it is
said, on the one hand, every moral principle is
tested and described by the circumstances which
surround its application. Also, in morals, it must
rest with every man at the crisis of action to determine his own course of conduct. On the other
hand, it is said, law must act in gross and to a

[41] In most of the cases allowing recovery there was a relation—
master and servant, *Hunicke v. Meremec Quarry Co.*, 262 Mo.
560; *Ohio R. Co. v. Early*, 141 Ind. 73; *Raasch v. Elite Laun-
dry Co.*, 98 Minn. 357; *Salter v. Nebraska Telephone Co.*, 79
Neb. 373; carrier and passenger, *Layne v. Chicago R. Co.*, 175
Mo. App. 35, 41. In case of seamen, it has always been recognized. *The Iroquois*, 194 U. S. 240; *Scarff v. Metcalf*, 107 N. Y.
211. For cases where there was no relation, see *Depue v. Flatau*,
100 Minn. 299; *Southern Ry. Co. v. Sewell*, 18 Ga. App. 544.
On the whole subject, see Bentham, *Principles of Morals and
Legislation*, 322-323; Bentham, *Works* (Bowring's ed.) I, 164;
Bentham, *Theory of Legislation* (Hildreth's transl. 5 ed.) 65-66;
Livingston, *Complete Works on Criminal Jurisprudence*, II, 126-
127; Macaulay, *Complete Works* (ed. 1875) VII, 493-497; *Dutch
Penal Code*, art. 450; *German Civil Code*, § 826; Liszt, *Die
Deliktsobligationen des Bürgerlichen Gesetzbuchs*, 72.

greater or less extent in the rough. Also, the law, so far as possible, seeks to leave nothing to doubt with respect to the lawfulness or unlawfulness of a course of conduct. If legal doubts exist at the crisis of action, it is considered a proof of defects in the law of the time and place. In the same spirit it is said that attempts to turn moral principles into detailed logical propositions lead to casuistry, while attempts to individualize the application of legal rules lead to arbitrary magisterial action and thus to oppression.[42]

We are not so sure of this opposition of law and morals with respect to application as we were in the nineteenth century. Thus in illustrating the distinction Amos says: "The same penalty for a broken law is exacted from persons of an indefinite number of shades of moral guilt."[43] He says this as if it showed conclusively that law would not take cognizance of the shades which morals would recognize. Probably his generation took the statement that the law does not recognize shades of guilt for axiomatic. But today, through administrative agencies and more enlightened penal treatment, the law is coming more and more to fit the treatment to the criminal and to do for individual offenders what had been as-

[42] Amos, *Science of Law*, 33-34.
[43] *Id.* 34.

sumed to be beyond the competency of legal administration of justice.[44] We have always had
some degree of individualized application of legal
precepts in courts of equity. Today the rise of
administrative tribunals and the growing tendency to commit subjects to them that were once
committed to the courts, bears witness to the demand for individualized application at many new
points. It will not do to say that our new régime
of administrative justice is not part of the law.

Nineteenth-century science of law assumed
that all legal rules were potentially in the jurist's
head, and were discovered by a purely logical
process. With the breakdown of this notion of
the finality of legal premises and logical existence
of all legal precepts from the beginning, much of
the significance of the supposed distinction in application between legal precepts and moral principles disappears. Rules of property, rules as to
commercial transactions, the rules that maintain
the security of acquisitions and the security of
transactions in a society of complex economic organization—such rules may be and ought to be of

---

[44] See *Relazione sul progetto preliminare di codice penale Itali-
ano*, I, 373-379; Barrows, *Indeterminate Sentence and the Parole
Law;* Miner, *Probation Work in the Magistrates' Courts of New
York City;* Henderson, *Penal and Reformatory Institutions;*
Brockway, *Fifty Years of Prison Service;* Leeson, *The Probation
System;* Lewis, *The Offender;* Herr, *Das moderne amerikanische
Besserungssystem.*

general and absolute application. But such rules
are not the whole of the law nor may they be
taken for the type of all legal precepts as the analytical jurist sought to do. Precepts for human
conduct, precepts determining for what conduct
one shall respond in civil proceedings and how he
shall respond, may admit of a very wide margin
of individualized application. Indeed in this connection the law often employs standards rather
than rules. In case of negligence the law applies
the standard of the conduct of a prudent man under the circumstances and puts it to the jury, in
effect as a moral proposition, to decide on their
individual notions of what is fair and reasonable
in the particular case. So in the Roman law,
where a standard of what a prudent husbandman
would do is applied to a usufructuary, or a standard of the conduct of a prudent and diligent head
of a family is applied to the parties to a transaction involving good faith. The opposition between law and morals with respect to application
is significant only in the law of property and in
commercial law—subjects that were to the fore
in the nineteenth century—and tends to disappear
in the law as to civil liability for action injurious
to others, the subject in which growth is going on
today.

It is equally a mistake to divorce the legal and the moral wholly, as the analytical jurists sought to do, and to identify them wholly as the natural-law jurists sought to do. For granting all that has been said as to the analytical distinction between law and morals with respect to subject matter and application, there remain three points at which ethical theory can be of little help to the jurist and with respect to which important areas in the law will have at least a non-moral character. In the first place, in order to maintain the social interest in the general security, to prevent conflict and to set up a legal order in the place of private war, the law must deal with many things which are morally indifferent. In many cases in the law of property and in the law of commercial transactions the law might require either of two alternative courses of action with equal justice, but must choose one and prescribe it in order to insure certainty. In such cases developed legal systems often exhibit the greatest diversity of detail. Usually the only moral element here is the moral obligation attaching to the legal precept merely as such, because of the social interest in the security of social institutions, of which law is one of the most fundamental. Aristotle pointed this out in his distinction between that which is just by nature or just in its idea and that which

derives its sole title to be just from convention or
enactment. The latter, he tells us, can be just
only with respect to those things which by nature
are indifferent.[45] This distinction, handed down
to modern legal science by Thomas Aquinas, has
become a commonplace of the philosophy of
law.[46] But we put it to grave misuse in our
conventional differentiation of *mala in se* from
mala prohibita; a doubtful distinction between
the traditionally anti-social, recognized and penalized as such in our historically given legal
materials, and recently penalized infringements
of newly or partially recognized social interests.
Aristotle was not speaking of crimes. He gives
as an example a law setting up an eponym for
a Greek city-state.[47] Recording acts, rules as to
the number of witnesses required for a will, as
to the words necessary to create estates, as to
the making, sealing. and delivery of deeds, and
the like, where the real desideratum is to have
a rule, to have it promulgated and as Bentham
would say "cognoscible"—such legal provisions

---

[45] *Nicomachean Ethics,* v, 7.

[46] Thomas Aquinas, *Summa Theologiae,* ii, 2, q. 57, art. 2; 1
Blackstone, *Commentaries,* 43.　See Pound, *Introduction to the
Philosophy of Law,* 25-26.

[47] "But the legal is that which originally was a matter of in-
difference, but which, when enacted, is so no longer; as the
price of ransom being fixed at a mina, or the sacrificing a goat
and not two sheep; and further all particular acts of legislation,
such as the sacrificing to Brasidas and all those matters which
are the subjects of decrees." *Nicomachean Ethics,* v, 7.

justify Aristotle's distinction. It is not a matter of morals whether we require two witnesses to a will or three. All that morals call for is that we have a certain, known rule and adhere to it.

Again, the law does not approve many things which it does not expressly condemn.[48] Many injuries are out of its reach. They are not susceptible of proof or they are inflicted by means too subtle or too intangible for the legal machinery of rule and sanction. Many interests must be left unsecured in whole or in part because they require too fine lines in their delimitation, or they are infringed by acts too intangible to admit of securing them by legal means. But it behooves the jurist to be vigilant in these cases. He should not assume too lightly that with progress in science and improved legal machinery the law will forever remain unable to do what it has been unable to do in the past. Such things as the hesitation of American courts to deal adequately with nervous illness caused by negligence without any bodily impact, using language of the past which is belied at every point by modern physiology and psychology, [49] or the reluctance of some courts to give adequate legal security to

----

[48] See Amos, *Science of Law*, 30; Pollock, *First Book of Jurisprudence* (4 ed.) 48-49.

[49] See Goodrich, *Emotional Disturbance and Legal Damage*, 20 Michigan Law Rev. 497.

personality, especially to the individual claim to privacy,[50] demonstrate the practical importance of insisting that our science of law shall not ignore morals. So long as for good reasons we cannot deal with such things legally, we must rest content. But we must not allow an analytical distinction between law and morals to blind us to the need of legal treatment of such cases whenever the onward march of human knowledge puts it in our power to treat them effectively.

Thirdly, law has to deal with cases of incidence of loss where both parties are morally blameless.[51] In such cases it may allow the loss to remain where it falls or it may seek to secure some social interest by changing the incidence of the loss. In such cases a large part of the legal difficulty arises from the very circumstance that the parties are equally blameless. Of late an "insurance theory" of liability has been urged for such situations. All of us, not merely the person who chances to be injured, should bear the losses incident to the operations of civilized society. Hence the law is to pass the loss on to all of us by way of imposing legal liability upon some one who is in a position to bear it in the first instance,

---

[50] See Pound, *Interests of Personality*, 28 Harvard Law Rev. 343, 362-364.

[51] Pollock, *First Book of Jurisprudence*, (4 ed.) 50-54.

and impose it ultimately upon the community in the way of charges for service rendered. Since the Workmen's Compensation Acts there has been a growing tendency in this direction.[52] But juristically these liabilities are always incident to some relation. Also the legislative reasons for imposing them have been primarily economic. Very likely the juristic and economic considerations may be given an ethical formulation. Nevertheless, I suspect that in this case ethics has followed jurisprudence, and that ethical theory does not help us here beyond recognizing the moral quality of obedience to the legal rule. Thus, *respondeat superior* is not a universal moral rule.[53] The shifting of the burden to the employer, no matter how careful he has been and how free from fault, proceeds on the social interest in the general security, which is maintained best by holding those who conduct enterprises in which others are employed to an absolute liability for what their servants do in the course of the enterprise.

---

[52] See, for example, the proposition to extend the principle of the workmen's compensation acts to railway accidents. Ballantine, *Modernizing Railway Accident Law* (reprinted from the Outlook of November 15, 1916).

[53] The various speculative justifications of the doctrine are criticized in Baty, *Vicarious Liability*, chap. VIII ("Justification in Ethics").

Such cases require definite rules in order to prevent arbitrary action by the magistrate. They differ from cases, such as negligence, where the moral quality of acts is to be judged with reference to a legally-fixed standard applied to the particular circumstances. In the latter, within wide limits, each trier of fact may have his own notion. In the former, this could not be tolerated. The most we can ask in the former is that our measure for maintaining the general security be not ethically objectionable. The moment we make a rule for a case of the former type we are not unlikely to provide a legal rule which is not a moral rule.

A closely related situation, which has given much difficulty, arises where both parties to a controversy have been at fault and the law must fix the incidence of loss in view of the culpability of each. It might be allowed to rest where it chanced to fall.[54] Or the whole might be cast

---

[54] "The reason of this rule is that, both parties being at fault, there can be no apportionment of the damages. . . The law does not justify or excuse the negligence of the defendant. It would, notwithstanding the negligence of the plaintiff, hold the defendant responsible, if it could. It merely allows him to escape judgment because, from the nature of the case, it is unable to ascertain what share of the damages is due to his negligence. He is both legally and morally to blame, but there is no standard by which the law can measure the consequences of his fault, and therefore only, he is allowed to go free of judgment." Sanderson, J., in *Needham v. San Francisco R. Co.*, 37 Cal. 409, 419. See also *Kerwhacker v. Cleveland R. Co.*, 3 Ohio St., 172, 188; *Heil v. Glanding*, 42 Pa. St. 493, 498.

on the one who is the more culpable, as by the doctrine of comparative negligence.[55] Or the whole might be cast on the one last culpable, as by the "last clear chance" doctrine[56] Or the loss might be divided or apportioned; either divided equally, or apportioned according to their respective culpability, as in the civil law and in admiralty.[57] If we had any machinery for the accurate quantitative or qualitative measurement of culpability in such cases, the latter would be required on ethical grounds. It is because all apportionment in such cases is theoretical, and at best arbitrary, that the law is troubled what to do. The fact that five doctrines have obtained on this subject and that American courts in the last century experimented with at least four of them speaks for itself.

In addition there is one general characteristic of law that makes for a certain opposition between the legal and the moral. The very conception of law involves ideas of uniformity, regularity, predicability. Administration of justice according to law is administration by legal precepts and chiefly by rule. But even the most flexible of

[55] Cooper, J., in *Louisville R. Co. v. Fleming,* 14 Lea (Tenn.) 128, 135; 1 Shearman and Redfield, *Negligence,* (6 ed.) §§ 102, 103.

[56] *Davies v. Mann,* 10 M. & W. 546.

[57] *The Max Morris,* 137 U. S. 1; Scott, *Collisions at Sea Where Both Ships Are in Fault,* 13 Law Quarterly Rev. 17.

mechanisms will operate more or less mechanically, and it is not easy to make legal machinery
flexible and at the same time adequate to the general security. The requirements of particular
cases must yield to the requirements of generality
and certainty in legal precepts and of uniformity
and equality in their application. Hence even
though in general the law tends to bring about
results accordant with the moral sense of the
community, the necessarily mechanical operation
of legal rules will in particular cases produce situations where the legal result and the result de-
manded by the moral sense of the community are
out of accord.[58] When such things happen it is
likely to be because of the survival of rules which
have merely a historical basis. But to a certain
extent they are an inevitable by-product of
justice according to law.

So much must be conceded to the analytical
jurist. Yet we must not omit to note that in the
last century he pressed these points too far.
Thus a writer upon ethics, who shows in marked
degree the effects of analytical jurisprudence,
says: "The law protects contracts which were
made in legitimate business without regard to
whether their provisions still conform to justice

[58] I have treated this more fully in a paper entitled *The Causes
of Popular Dissatisfaction with the Administration of Justice*, 29
Rep. Am. Bar Assn., 395, 397-398.

or not. Owing to unforseen circumstances things
may so have changed as to cause the ruin of one
of the contracting parties should the contract now
be carried out, perhaps without substantially
benefitting the other party. The law is not concerned with that."[59] The proposition is true of
the strict law, although in practice in such a case
it might not be easy to find a jury that would give
an adequate value to the bargain in its verdict in
an action for damages. But when the promisee
went into equity for his only effective and adequate remedy (specific performance) he would
encounter the chancellor's margin of discretion in
the application of that remedy and the doctrine
that supervening circumstances may make a bargain so hard that the court will refuse to enforce
it.[60] In other words, the law in action is not as
bad as the author would have us believe.

And yet there are too many points, such, for
example, as the law with respect to promises made
in the course of business but without a tech-

---

[59] Paulsen, *Ethics,* (Thilly's transl.) 629. The influence of
Jhering on Paulsen's views as to the relation of law and morals
is manifest. Hence his position is substantially that of the
analytical jurists. *Ethics,* (Thilly's transl.) 624-637.

[60] See *Willard v. Tayloe,* 8 Wall. 557. In the civil law such
cases are provided for by administrative *moratoria*. Thaller,
Traité élémentaire de droit commerciel (6 ed.) §§ 1515 ff. Compare the *beneficium competentiae* in Roman law, Dig. xlii, 1, 16-17,
xlii, 1, 19, § 1, l, 17, 173; Baudry-Lacantinerie, *Précis de droit
civil,* (11 ed.) I, § 529; and in American legislation limitations
on the power of creditors to exact satisfaction. Thompson, *Home-
steads and Exemptions,* §§ 40, 379.

nical consideration, where we have not exerted
ourselves as we should have done to bring the
legal and the moral into accord.[61]   The philo-
ical jurist was too prone to find ingenious
philosophical justification for rules and doctrines
and institutions which had outlived the conditions
for which they arose and had ceased to yield just
results.   The historical jurist was too prone to
find a justification for an arbitrary rule in the
fact that it was the culmination of a historical
development.   The analytical jurist banished all
ethical considerations, all criticism of legal precepts with reference to morals, from the law
books.   If the precept could be fitted logically
into a logically consistent legal system, it was
enough.   Such things are intelligible as a reaction from extravagances of the law-of-nature
school.   They are intelligible also in a stage of
legal development, following a period of growth,
when it was expedient for a time to assimilate
and systematize the results of creative judicial
and juristic activity.   Moreover, the latter part of
the nineteenth century was not a constructive era
in any of the sciences.   A physicist said recently:
"Rapid progress was not characteristic of the latter half of the nineteenth century—at least not in

---

[61] I have discussed this fully in *An Introduction to the Phi
losophy of Law*, lect. 6, especially 267-284.

physics. Fine, solid, dynamical foundations were laid, and the edifice of knowledge was consolidated; but wholly fresh ground was not being opened up, and totally new buildings were not expected."[62]

Today we are seeing the beginning of a reaction from the juristic pessimism of the historical school and the juristic inertia of the later generations of the analytical school. The work of systematizing the received body of legal precepts and discovering its logical presuppositions by analysis has been done. The pressure of new and unsecured interests, of new and insistent human claims, is compelling us to revise our juristic creeds. Projects for "restatement of the law" are in the air. Jurists are becoming more confident of the efficacy of intelligent effort to improve the law. Already there is a revival of natural law—not of the natural law that would have imposed upon us an idealized version of the law of the past as something from which we might never escape, but of a creative natural law that would enable us to make of our received legal materials, as systematized by the legal science of the last century, a living instrument of justice in the society of today and of tomorrow. Such a natural law will not call upon us to turn treatises on

---

[62] Lodge, *Continuity*, 4 (1914).

ethics or economics or sociology directly into institutes of law. But it will not be content with a legal science that refuses to look beyond or behind formal legal precepts and so misses more than half of what goes to make up the law. It will not be content to justify legal precepts by an ideal form of themselves. It will not be content with a jurisprudence that excludes the ends of law and criticism of legal precepts with reference to those ends.

III

THE PHILOSOPHICAL VIEW

Throughout the nineteenth century philosophical jurists devoted much of their attention to the relation of law to morals, the relation of jurisprudence to ethics. For reasons considered in a preceding lecture the subject was not congenial to the legal science of the time, which sought to be wholly self-sufficient, using its own methods exclusively and applying them exclusively to rigidly defined legal materials. Also much of the discussion was none too happy, so that Jhering could say that the relation of law to morals was the Cape Horn of jurisprudence; the juristic navigator who would overcome its perils ran no little risk of fatal shipwreck.[1] In English and American writing the subject was embarrassed further by the circumstance that the arguments were largely taken over from the German metaphysical jurists who used words to which our "law" and "morals" by no means exactly correspond. The Germans were discussing the relation of *Recht* to *Sitte;* and *Recht* is more

---

[1] *Geist des römischen Rechts,* II, § 26 (2 ed.) 46. See comments on this in Ahrens, *Naturrecht,* (6 ed.) I, 308.

than "law" in our conventional, analytical sense, while *Sitte* implies more than "morals." *Recht* is "right and law"—the law looked at not merely as courts enforce it, but also with reference to what the courts are seeking to attain through the judicial administration of justice. *Sitte* means more than morals in the sense in which we commonly use the term.[2] It implies habits of mind—those principles of conduct in civilized society which have become second nature and of which we are not always conscious. It might be called ethical custom. In other words, the problem which we translate as the relation of law to morals was, to those who began the discussion and chiefly prosecuted it, this : Is that which the legal order is trying immediately to attain identical with ethical custom or is it something to be differentiated from ethical custom and set over against it? It is a philosophical version of the problem of the relation of law to custom which was debated at the same time by analytical and historical jurists.

As we have seen, philosophy of law begins in a stage of legal development in which law is relatively undifferentiated from general social control; in which law and ethical custom and

---

[2] This is well explained in Haldane, *Higher Nationality: A Study in Law and Ethics*, 38 Rep. Am. Bar Assn., 393, 402-405.

traditional customs of popular action and religious observance are fused or undifferentiated. Philosophy of law begins by attempting to find the ideal side, the enduring idea, of social control. The philosophy of social control is taken up by Roman lawyers in a stage of legal growth, after a period of strict law, and becomes philosophical jurisprudence—an attempt to find the ideal side, the enduring idea, of law and of each legal rule and institution and doctrine, and thus to find an ideal body of law by which to try, and from which to eke out, the legal materials handed down from the old Roman city-state. This philosophical jurisprudence is revived and carried forward through a rationalist philosophy of law in the corresponding stage of development in the modern world. Thus, it has its origin in a stage in which law, morals, ethical custom and religious usage are undifferentiated. It becomes the prevailing method of the science of law in stages of growth in which a large infusion of morals or of ethical custom into law is going forward. Hence it is invoked at the outset to give a rational account of that infusion and does so by assuming the ultimate identity of legal rules with moral rules.

When we add to these circumstances, which gave form to philosophical thought about law in the periods in which men were using philosophy as an everyday instrument of creative legal development, the further circumstance that jurisprudence had been a part of theology for two centuries prior to the Reformation, we may understand the fundamental assumptions of the classical philosophical jurisprudence of the law-of-nature school. We may perceive why jurisprudence was regarded as a branch of ethics and why legal rules were held only declaratory of moral rules. We may see why it was conceived that a rule could not be a valid legal rule unless it was a moral rule—not merely that it ought not to be a legal rule if it ran counter to a moral rule—and why it was assumed that moral rules as such were legally obligatory.

Had the seventeenth and eighteenth-century jurisprudence urged that positive law got its validity from being declaratory of ethical custom of the time and place—or perhaps better from being declaratory of idealized ethical custom of the time and place—it would not have broken down so completely at the end of the eighteenth century. But the rationalist philosophy of the time was not inclined to so modest a proposition.

Moreover the political controversies of the time
led to a political ethics in which, setting the individual and the state and so the individual and
society over against one another, the basis of
political and legal obligation was found in the
appeal of political institutions and legal precepts
to the individual conscience as being such as
would bind an abstract man in a state of perfection—such as would bind him as a moral entity
in a state in which he would claim nothing and
do nothing that did not comport with ideal moral
perfection.[3]

In juristic practice natural law came to no more
than the more modest conception of an ethically
idealized law of the time and place or ethically

---

[3] "It is proper to observe in this connection that when we speak
of the natural state of man we are to understand not only that
natural and primitive state in which he is placed, as it were, by
the hands of nature herself, but as well all those into which man
enters by his own act and agreement, that are on the whole in
accord with his nature and that contain nothing but what is
agreeable to his constitution and to the end for which he was
formed. For since man, as a free and intelligent being, is able
to see and know his situation and to discover his ultimate end,
and hence to take the right measures to attain it, in order to
form a just idea of his natural state, we must consider it in
this light. That is, to speak generally, the natural state of man
is that which is conformable to his nature, constitution and reason, as well as to the good use of his faculties, considered in
their full maturity and perfection." Burlamaqui, *Principes du
droit naturel*, I, 4, § 10.
    "Man is a moral person, when looked at as the subject of cer-
tain duties and certain rights. Hence his state, which is determined by duties and rights, is called moral; this state is also
called natural, where the duties and rights by which it is determined are natural or belong to it by the force of the law of
nature. And therefore in the natural state men are governed
solely by the law of nature." Wolff, *Institutiones Iuris Naturae
et Gentium*, § 96.

idealized Roman law, supplemented by an ethical
ideal of the end of law. Such was the natural
law that liberalized the legal materials that had
come down from the Middle Ages and brought
the law abreast of morals or ethical custom. But
the theory went much further, and in the latter
part of the eighteenth century its implications
were anti-social. For in effect it made the individual conscience the ultimate arbiter of political
and legal obligations.[4] Thus Mr. Justice Wilson
says: "No exterior human authority can bind a
free and independent man."[5] Also: "The consent of those whose obedience the law requires
. . . I conceive to be the true origin of the
obligation of human laws."[6] Jefferson's pronouncements to the same effect are well known,[7]
Such a doctrine could be tolerable in practice only
in a time when absolute theories of morals prevailed. They assume, indeed, a standard conscience—as it were, a conscientious man's conscience, analogous to the prudence of the reasonable man in our law of torts. It is not every

---

[4] Burlamaqui, II, 3, c. 1, § 6; Wolff, § 1069; Vattel, *Le droit
des gens,* liv. I, ch. 13, § 159; 1 Blackstone, *Commentaries,* 41.

[5] *Works,* (Andrews' ed.) I, 192.

[6] Id. 88. See also 57, 190, 198.

[7] E.g., Letter to James Madison, September 6, 1789, *Writings*
(Ford's ed.) V, 115-124; Letter to Samuel Kerchevall, Id. X, 37,
42-45.

man's conscience as his wilful pursuit of the
desires of the moment makes it appear, but the
real conscience that he has as a rational moral
entity, which is the measure of the obligatory
force of legal rules.

For example, the "right of revolution" so much
discussed by eighteenth-century jurists, a principle, says Mr. Justice Wilson, which "should be
taught as a principle of the constitution of the
United States and of every state in the Union,"[8]
can be admitted, as something to be left to the
conscience of every individual for the occasion
and the manner of its exercise, only when all
men or most men are agreed. On a balance of
the security of social institutions and the individual life it may not be anti-social to overturn
social institutions that have become anti-social in
their operation and effect. But here again the
natural-law theory did not put it so modestly.
And it was only agreement in looking to some
ultimate authority for decisive pronouncement on
the content and application of moral principles
that made the theory possible. There was a general agreement upon ethical custom. It could be
assumed that every individual in a homogeneous
community with a relatively simple economic

---

[8] *Works* (Andrews' ed.) I, 18.

organization felt as did his fellows with respect
to "things that are not done." If John Doe or
Richard Roe asserted that their respective consciences did not dictate or approve the rules
which the philosophical jurist found in his own
conscience and attributed to the conscience of
man in a state of nature, it meant simply that
John and Richard were ignorant of the dictates
of their consciences or were misrepresenting
them. Only in this way could the individualist
political natural law of the eighteenth century be
made compatible with the general security.[9]

Nor was the classical natural-law theory less
vulnerable on its juristic than on its political side.
It came practically to this, that each philosophical
jurist made his personal ethical views the test of
the validity of legal precepts and the pattern for
new precepts or for new shapings of old ones.
So long as men were agreed as to the main features of ethical custom, this mode of thought was
a powerful agency of growth. It led each jurist
to work out ideal standards to serve as a critique
of the traditional law in every detail. It led to
many a bold stroke for judicial improvement of
the common law and not the least to the enlightened creative decisions of Lord Mansfield and

---

[9] See Brown, *Underlying Principles of Modern Legislation*,
7 ff.; Ritchie, *Natural Rights*, 65 ff.

his colleagues. And yet it had too much of the personal in it, in action, to survive the shocks of the end of the century when it appeared that men were by no means all agreed upon ethical principles or ethical custom, and natural-law theories, applied to political and legal institutions in paper constitutions and codes drawn up as if there had been no legal past, threatened what might be called institutional waste.[10]

In the hands of Pothier natural law was of much service to the modern law of Continental Europe in leading him to lay down that deliberate promises, being morally binding, were legally binding, although they did not come within the Roman categories of contract, since the Roman categories were arbitrary and remote from natural simplicity.[11] It rendered notable service in

---

[10] "But one of the first and most leading principles on which the commonwealth and the laws are consecrated, is lest the temporary possessors and life-renters in it, unmindful of what they have received from their ancestors, or of what is due to their posterity, should act as if they were the entire masters; that they should not think it amongst their rights to cut off the entail or commit waste on the inheritance, by destroying at their pleasure the whole original fabric of their society; hazarding to leave to those who come after them a ruin instead of a habitation, and teaching these successors as little to respect their contrivances as they had themselves respected the institutions of their forefathers." Burke, Reflections on the Revolution in France, *Works*, (1839 ed.) III, 118. See also 110-111, 118-121.

[11] "That kind of agreement the object of which is the formation of an engagement is called a contract. The principles of the Roman law as to the different kinds of agreements, and the distinction between contracts and simple agreements, not being founded on the law of nature, and being indeed very remote from simplicity, are not admitted into our law." *Traité des obligations*, pt. I, ch. 1, sect. 1, art. 1, § 1, *Oeuvres* (3 ed.) II, 4.

the hands of Lord Mansfield leading him in commercial cases, instead of leaving each case to a jury to decide upon the fact of commercial custom, to study "to find some general principle, which shall be known to all mankind, not only to rule the particular case then under consideration, but to serve as a guide for the future." [12] On the other hand, it led to ignorings of the history of legal precepts by the codifiers with resulting exhibitions of mistaken legislative zeal that prejudiced jurists against codes for nearly a century. [13] Its possibilities in the hands of lawyers of lesser magnitude are illustrated in the New York Journeymen Cordwainers' Case in which, in a prosecution for a common-law misdemeanor, it was argued that the common-law doctrine did not obtain in America, since "whether it is not an attack upon the rights of man is . . . more fitting to be inquired into than whether or not it is conformable to the usages of Picts, Romans, Britons, Danes, Jutes, Angles, Saxons, Normans, or other barbarians who lived in the night of human intelligence." [14]

---

[12] Buller, J., in *Lickbarrow* v. *Mason*, 2 T. R. 63, 73.

[13] See Savigny, *Vom Beruf unsrer Zeit für Gesetzgebung und Rechtswissenschaft* (3 ed.) 32-151; Savigny, *System des heutigen römischen Rechts*, II, § 75 (Rattigan's transl. Savigny, Jural Relations, 111-119); Austin, *Jurisprudence*, (4 ed.) II, 689-697.

[14] Yates' *Select Cases*, 111, 156.

Bentham pointed out the weak point in the classical natural law in a famous passage. Speaking of the various proposed criteria for distinguishing between right and wrong, he says they "consist in so many contrivances for avoiding the obligation of appealing to any external standard and of prevailing upon the reader to accept of the author's sentiment or opinion as a reason for itself." He then discusses eight of these "contrivances" and adds: "The fairest and openest of them all is that sort of man who speaks out and says, I am of the number of the elect; now God himself takes care to inform the elect what is right, and that with so good effect . . . they cannot help . . . knowing it. . . . If, therefore, a man wants to know what is right he has nothing to do but to come to me."[15]

A few examples will show that Bentham's statement is not in the least overdrawn. An American judge, expounding natural limitations upon lawmaking said that "no court . . . would hesitate to declare void a statute which enacted that A and B, who were husband and wife to each other, should be so no longer, but that A should thereafter be the husband of C,

---

[15] *Principles of Morals and Legislation* (Clarendon Press reprint), note on pp. 17-20.

and B the wife of D."[16]   On the other hand,
Lord Holt, approving the doctrine of Coke that
"when an act of Parliament is against common
right and reason . . . the common law will
control it and adjudge such act to be void," says
that Parliament may not make adultery lawful
but that it may enact that B shall no longer be
the wife of A but shall instead be the wife of C.[17]
What this means is that the American judge took
our state constitutional provisions as to the separation of powers, and consequent prohibitions of
legislative divorce, to be declaratory of natural
law, while the English judge was familiar with
parliamentary divorce as an everyday matter and
hence assumed that the natural-law limitation
upon legislative action did not extend thereto.

Again, in *Dred Scott* v. *Sanford,* assuming
apparently that Lord Mansfield's statement of
English law of the last half of the eighteenth
century[18] was declaratory of natural law, Mr.
Justice Curtis asserts dogmatically that slavery
cannot exist except as a creature of municipal
law, and adds that such is the opinion of all

---

[16] Miller, J., in *Loan Ass'n.* v. *Topeka,* 20 Wall. 655, 662-663.
[17] *City of London* v. *Wood,* 12 Mod. 669, 687-688.
[18] "The state of slavery is of such a nature that it is incapable
of being introduced on any reasons, moral or political, but only
by positive law, which preserves its force long after the reasons,
occasion and time itself, from whence it was created, is erased
from memory." 20 *State Trials,* 1, 82.

writers.[19]   Yet Aristotle,[20] Grotius[21] and Ruth-
erforth,[22] no mean authorities upon natural law,
make elaborate arguments to prove that in certain
cases slavery may have a natural foundation.
Natural law of the eighteenth-century kind did
not need to trouble about authorities. The
author's reason and conscience could tell him
what was natural law and no rational authority
could conceivably disagree. One cannot but see
that the circumstance that the one wrote where
slavery had long ceased to exist, while the others
were familiar with it as an institution, had
decisive effect upon the dictates of reason.

An eighteenth-century jurist laying down natural law and Bentham's man who claimed to be
one of the elect are in the same position. Each is
giving us his personal views and is assuming that

---

[19] "Slavery, being contrary to natural right, is created only by
municipal law. This is not only plain in itself, and agreed by all
writers on the subject, but is inferable from the constitution and
has been explicitly declared by this court." *Dred Scott* v. *Sand-
ford,* 19 How. 393, 624.

[20] "But is there any one thus intended by nature to be a slave,
and for whom such a condition is expedient and right, or rather
is not all slavery a violation of nature? There is no difficulty in
answering this question, on grounds both of reason and of fact.
For that some should rule, and others be ruled, is a thing not
only necessary but expedient; from the hour of their birth, some
are marked out for subjection, others for rule. . . . It is
clear, then, that some men are by nature free, and others slaves,
and that for these latter slavery is both expedient and right."
Politics, i, ch. 5 (Jowett's transl. I, 7-8).

[21] *De jure belli ac pacis,* 1, 5, 27, § 2; I, 5, 29, §§ 1-2.
Whewell's transl. I, 333-334, 335-336

[22] *Institutes of Natural Law,* I, 20, § 4.

those views must be binding upon everyone else. When and where absolute theories of morals prevail, upon the main features of which all or substantially all are agreed, a jurist may use the generally accepted picture of what is right as a pattern for constructive work upon legal materials. From such a source authoritative natural law may be drawn in any quantity without impairing the general security. Under such circumstances it is possible to realize Bentham's man who was one of the elect. But when absolute theories have been discarded and no authorities are recognized universally, and especially when classes with divergent claims and desires hold diverse views on fundamental points, natural law in the eighteenth-century sense would make every man a law unto himself. The application of natural-law theories by revolutionary France made men conscious of this and led Burke in politics,[23] Cuoco in political history,[24] and Savigny in jurisprudence[25] to break with the philosophical method of the past two centuries and found the historical political science and his-

---

[23] See Laski, *English Political Thought from Locke to Bentham*, 243-256; Braune, *Edmund Burke in Deutschland*.

[24] *Saggio storico*, §§ 1-7 (1800). See Croce, *Storia della storiografia Italiana nel secolo decimomono*, I, 11.

[25] See Pound, *Interpretations of Legal History*, 12-14. Compare the attitude of Maine toward these same ideas as urged by the neo-Rousseauists, *Popular Government*, (American ed.) 154-162.

torical jurisprudence of the nineteenth century. Also the nineteenth century philosophical, or, as we may call them, metaphysical, jurists sought to ground natural law upon some fundamental conception, given us independently and having an absolute and universal validity.

As a result for about one hundred years philosophers and philosophical jurists, instead of conceiving of legal precepts as declaring and promulgating moral principles, sought to set apart and to contrast the legal and the moral.

Kant, whose influence upon the analytical jurists was remarked in the preceding lecture, began by saying that man, in endeavoring to bring his animal self and his rational self into harmony, was presented to himself in two aspects, an inner and an outer. Hence his acts have a twofold aspect. On the one hand, they are external manifestations of his will. On the other hand, they are determinations of his will by motives. On the one hand, he is in relation to other beings like himself and to things external. On the other hand he is, as it were, alone with himself. The law has to do with his acts in the one aspect. Morals have to do with them in the other aspect. The problem of the law is to keep conscious free-willing beings from interference with each other.

It is so to order them that each shall exercise his
freedom in a way consistent with the freedom of
all others, since all others are to be regarded
equally as ends in themselves. But law has to do
with outward acts. Hence it reaches no further
than the possibility of outward compulsion. In a
legal sense there is a right only to the extent that
others may be compelled to respect it.[26]

To quote Kant's own words: "When it is said
that a creditor has the right to exact payment
from his debtor, it does not mean that he may
put it to the debtor's conscience that the latter
ought to pay. It means that in such a case payment may be compelled consistently with the
freedom of everyone and hence consistently with
the debtor's own freedom, according to a universal law."[27]   And this may happen sometimes
even though from the internal aspect of demand-
ing performance one ought not to do so. One
example which he discusses is suggestive. There
was a much-controverted text in the Prussian
Code of Frederick the Great dealing with the
case where changes in the monetary system had
taken place between the creation and the maturity
of a debt. Was payment to be made according

---

[26] *Metaphysische Anfangsgründe der Rechtslehre,* Intr. §§ B-D.
See Caird, *The Critical Philosophy of Kant,* II, 294-300.
[27] *Metaphysische Anfangsgründe der Rechtslehre,* (2 ed.) xxxvi.

to the current value or the metallic value or the nominal value?[28] Kant answers, from the standpoint of the correspondence of claim to compel with right: "When the currency in which it is covenanted that a debt should be paid has become depreciated in the interval between the covenant and the payment, the creditor may have an equitable claim to be reimbursed; but it is impossible that a judge should enforce it, seeing the creditor has got that for which he bargained and nothing was said in the contract of such a contingency."[29] Thus there is an equitable or moral claim which is not a right from the standpoint of an ideal legal order. Kant's solution is much in the spirit of the strict law and hence of the maturity of law, which has many affinities thereto. It is noteworthy that Anglo-American equity, which in spite of nineteenth-century attempts to systematize it to the pattern of the strict law, has preserved much of the spirit of seventeenth-century identification of law and morals, refuses to enforce hard bargains where they have become hard because of unforeseen changes in the value of money.[30] Kant's solution accords with the result

---

[28] Savigny, *Obligationenrecht,* § 46. Brown, *Epitome and Analysis of Savigny on Obligations,* 81-82.

[29] *Metaphysische Anfangsgründe der Rechtslehre,* (2 ed.) xxxix-xl. I have quoted Caird's paraphrase-translation, *Critical Philosophy of Kant,* II, 299.

[30] *Willard* v. *Tayloe,* 8 Wall. 557.

generally reached by legal systems today. Indeed,
in American law although the creditor cannot
enforce specific performance in such a case, he
can recover the value of his bargain in an action
at law.[31] Hence all that is achieved by the refusal
of equity to interfere is that the creditor is left
to what is often a much less adequate remedy.
The chancellor washes his hands of the matter
and says, "go to a court of law where they are
more callous."

In Kant's theory law and morals are distinguished. Indeed long before him Thomasius had
begun to insist on the distinction, coincident with
the legislative movement and codifying tendency
that led to an idea of positive law as an authoritatively imposed declaration of natural law by a
superior reason, and hence to an imperative
theory of its obligation.[32] In the maturity of law
in the nineteenth century the same circumstances
that led analytical jurists to adopt this distinction
between law and morals and to carry it still
further, led to philosophical attempts to express
the relation of law and morals by contrasting
them. Thus Hegel represents the relation as an

---

[31] Such is the prevailing doctrine in the United States. For the
different rules see 3 Sedgwick, *Damages* (9 ed.) §§ 1001-1012.
    [32]*Fundamenta iuris naturae et gentium,* I, 1, 6, §§ 3, 32-43,
64-66, 74-75, I, 1, 4, §§ 89-91, I, 1, 5, § 47; *Institutiones juris-
prudentiae divinae* (7 ed.) I, 2, §§ 63-100.

antithesis. Right, that is, that which we seek to attain through law, is the possibility of liberty. Morals determine not what is possible but what ought to be. Hence law and morals are in contrast to each other as the possible (i. e., possible of external realization) and the internally obligatory.[33] Ahrens contrasts them also. Both are deductions from a fundamental conception of right or of justice, but they differ in that in the case of morals our deductions give us a subjective science while in law they give us an objective science. In morals our deductions are with reference to the motives of conduct; in law they are with reference to the outward results of conduct. The spheres are different and in consequence the content of the two spheres may well be different likewise.[34]

In the latter part of the nineteenth century, as individualistic theories, proceeding on the ultimate datum of the free-willing conscious individual, begin to give way to theories which proceed not upon a first principle of individual independence but upon the basis of the social interde-

---

[33] *Grundlinien der Philosophie des Rechts,* §§ 104-114. See Reyburn, *Hegel's Ethical Theory,* 118-121; Wallace, *Hegel's Philosophy of Mind,* 21-23.

[34] *Cours de droit naturel,* (8 ed.) I, § 21. As to the relation of this to Krause, see Id. 78-80.

pendence of men, attempts to contrast law and morals are given up and we come upon a new phase of attempts to subordinate law to morals.

Toward the end of the nineteenth century a new movement became manifest in law and in the science of law. Faith in the spontaneous development of legal institutions began to give way to faith in the efficacy of effort to make or to shape the law to known ends. A tendency arose to direct legal as well as political institutions consciously to the furtherance of general human ends, instead of restricting their operation to a few supposedly paramount ends. In particular, whereas the immediate past had put the whole emphasis upon the general security, greater weight began to be given to the individual human life. Just as the maturity of law reverted in some measure to the spirit and the ideas of the strict law, this new tendency began to have much in common with the stage of infusion of lay moral ideas into law which may be called the stage of equity and natural law. In jurisprudence it was manifest first in a better understanding of the relation of legal rights to so-called natural rights. It came to be seen that the ultimate thing was the claim or demand or desire of a human being; that out of all such *de facto* claims or demands or desires some were recognized by ethical customs, some were recognized by moralists and jurists as reasonable and were called natural rights, and some were recognized and delimited by law and as so delimited were given effect by legal rights. In legislation and judicial decision it has been manifest in a steady movement since the end of the last century in quite another direction from that taken in what I have called the maturity of law. Emphasis has been transferring from individual interests to social interests. Satisfaction of human wants has been the watchword rather than general security. Instead of setting law off from all other social institutions we have been coördinating it with them in an endeavor through all of them to satisfy as much of human wants as we may with the least sacrifice.[35]

Along with this movement there has gone a revival of philosophy of law, through the rise of a social philosophical school of many types in place of the metaphysical school of the last cen-

---

[35] I have considered this movement at large on other occasions: *The Scope and Purpose of Sociological Jurisprudence,* 35 Harvard Law Rev. 489, 506-516; *The End of Law as Developed in Legal Rules and Doctrines,* 27 Harvard Law Rev. 195, 225-234; *The Spirit of the Common Law,* lect. 8. See also Ehrlich, *Grundlegung der Soziologie des Rechts,* chaps. 9-10.

tury. And one feature of this revival has been new theories of legal precepts as having for their end the realization of moral rules, and in consequence a revival of the old subordination of jurisprudence to ethics.

As far back as 1878 Jellinek made the transition from a contrasting of law and morals to a subsuming of the former under the latter. Law, he said, was a minimum ethics. That is, the field of law was that part of the requirements of morals observance whereof is absolutely indispensable in the given stage of social development. By "law" here *(Recht)* he meant law as what we try to make it or in its idea: for the actual body of legal precepts may fall short of or in places or at times may go beyond this ethical minimum. So regarded, law is only a part of morals—i. e., the field of law is only a part of the field of ethical custom—namely, the part which has to do with the indispensable conditions of the social order. In the broader sense, morals include the whole. But in the narrower sense, as distinguished from law, they include only the excess beyond the indispensable minimum. This excess, which is desirable but not indispensable, he terms "an ethical luxury." The minimum represents what we may expect to give effect through legal precepts.[36] Law and morals are contrasted and yet in a broader sense morals are made to embrace the whole. This is significant. In other respects the theory has characteristic features of the nineteenth century. For example, it assumes that the scope of the law is to be held down to the smallest area possible. This is a legacy of the metaphysical jurisprudence which derived everything from the free will. Regarded as a systematic restriction of freedom in the interest of a maximum of individual free self-assertion, law was necessary and yet in some sort an evil. It was to be scrutinized jealously and was not to be suffered to extend itself beyond what was obviously necessary.[37] The chief value of Jellinek's work was in directing our attention to the psychological limitations upon effective legal ac-

---

[36] *Die sozialethische Bedeutung von Recht, Unrecht und Strafe,* chap. 2. Demogue, *Les notions fondamentales du droit privé,* 13 ff. "The endeavor to find any other difference between law and morals, and especially between customary law and ethical custom, than a higher or lesser importance for the ordering of the common life, has not thus far proved successful." Radbruch, *Einführung in die Rechtswissenschaft,* 11-12.

[37] "Reduced to these terms the difference between morality and right (i.e., *diritto*—right plus law) is a difference in degree and not of essence. Yet it is a very important difference, as it reduces the power of coercion to what is absolutely necessary for the harmonious coexistence of the individual with the whole." Lioy, *Philosophy of Right,* (transl. by Hastie) I, 121.

tion which often may preclude us from achieving by legal machinery and legal sanctions what on moral grounds we are moved to attempt.[38]

In one form or another a tendency to subordinate philosophical jurisprudence to ethics appears in all the types of the social philosophical school. As the social utilitarians put it, the immediate end of law is to secure interests, that is, to secure human claims or demands. Accordingly, we must choose which we shall recognize, must fix the limits within which we shall recognize them, and must weigh or evaluate conflicting or overlapping interests in order to secure as much as we may with the least sacrifice. In making this choice and in weighing or evaluating interests, whether in legislation or judicial decision or juristic writing, whether we do it by lawmaking or in the application of law, we must turn to ethics for principles. Morals is an evaluation of interests; law is or at least seeks to be a delimitation in accordance therewith.[39]   Thus we are

---

[38] *Allgemeine Staatslehre* (2 ed.) 89 ff., 324 ff. "Law is too costly to be used to enforce the whole moral law." Parsons, *Legal Doctrine and Social Progress*, 19.

[39] Korkunov, *General Theory of Law* (transl. by Hastings) 52. "The idea of value is, therefore, the basal conception of ethics. No other term, such as duty, law, or right, is final for thought; each logically demands the idea of value as the foundation upon which it finally rests. One may ask, when facing some apparent claim of morality, 'why is this my duty, why must I obey this law, or why regard this course of action as right?' The answer to any of these questions consists in showing that the require-

brought back in substance to a conception of jurisprudence as on one side a branch of applied ethics.

As the leader of the Neo-Kantians put it, we seek justice through law. But to attain justice through law we must formulate the ideals of the epoch. Even if we cannot formulate social and political and jural ideals so as to fix the details or at least the main lines of an immutable natural law that shall stand fast forever, we may make the legal administration of justice advance and give effect to the ideals of the time and place. Thus we may at least have a natural law with a growing content—an idealized ethical custom and an ideal picture of the end of law, painted, it may be, with reference to the institutions and ethical custom of the time and place, which may serve as an instrument of shaping and developing legal materials and of drawing in and fashioning materials from outside of the law.[40]   But these

---

ments of duty, law, and right tend in each case to promote human welfare, to yield what men do actually find to be of value." Everett, *Moral Values*, 7.

[40] "Hence the old jurists were wrong when they sought for a determinate law of absolute significance. But they would have been on firm ground if they had striven for a natural law with changing content—that is, precepts of right and law which contain a theoretically just law under relations empirically conditioned." Stammler, *Wirthschaft und Recht*, (2 ed.) 181. See Stammler, *Lehre von dem richtigen Rechte*, 116-121; Charmont, *La renaissance du droit naturel*, chap. 9 (Modern French Legal Philosophy, 106-111); Saleilles, *L'école historique et droit naturel, Revue trimestrielle de droit civil*, I, 80, 98; Demogue, *Notions fondamentales du droit privé*, 22.

ideals are developed outside of the law. They are moral ideals. And so jurisprudence is subordinated to ethics, in so far as ethics has to do with these goals which we seek to attain and with reference whereto we measure legal precepts and doctrines and institutions, in the endeavor to make them agencies of progress toward these goals, while jurisprudence has to do rather with the means of attaining them.

As the leader of the Neo-Hegelians put it, government, law, and morals in the sense of ethical custom, are factors toward the attainment of an ideal of civilization. So, he tells us, jurisprudence must appreciate the ideal ends toward which society strives.[41] Perhaps he alone of the leaders of recent philosophical jurisprudence did not more or less avowedly go back in some degree to the subordination of jurisprudence to ethics. His view was evolutionary. Law and morals express and also further a progressive civilization.[42] Hence jurisprudence and ethics are both subordinated to a universal history of civilization from which we determine the course of development of civilization, and to a philosophy of right and of economics from which we determine the jural

---

[41] *Moderne Rechtsprobleme*, §§ 1-7; *Rechtsphilosophie und Universalrechtsgeschichte*, § 9.

[42] Kohler, *Lehrbuch der Rechtsphilosophie*, 2.

postulates of the civilization of the time and place.[43] More than one recent book on ethics, however, presupposes very nearly what he called for, and the result in practice is to make jurisprudence more or less dependent on a science which a type of modern ethical philosophers would be likely to claim as theirs.

If we review the course of development of legal philosophical theory as to law and morals in connection with the development of legal precepts and legal institutions, we shall see at once that the philosophical theories bear a close relation to the actual legal phenomena of the time and place. Indeed they are little more than attempts to give a rational account of the problems of the legal order in different stages of development, and of the means by which those problems are solving. In the first stage law and morals are largely undifferentiated, and we get theories of the just by nature and the just by convention as explanations of local variations of ethical custom and law. In the stage of the strict law the legal precepts are self-sufficient and nothing of consequence is taken over from without. Morals are ignored and philosophy is called on to do no more than to provide or to bolster up an authoritative

---

[43] *Ibid. Rechtsphilosophie und Universalrechtsgeschichte,* § 2

foundation. In the stage of equity or natural law
the received body of legal precepts is no longer
self-sufficient. The pressure of unsecured interests and of ignored ethical custom leads to a large
infusion of moral ideas from without. Hence
for a time morals are chiefly regarded, and philosophical jurists think of legal rules as one sort
of moral rules and subordinate jurisprudence to
ethics. When the infusion is complete and the
pressure has abated so that the task for a time is
one of assimilation and systematization of what
has been taken over, questions of morals seem to
be only for the legislator, in the exceptional cases
where his intervention is required, and so law and
morals, jurisprudence and ethics, are coördinated
or contrasted. Finally in the beginning of a new
stage of growth, when unsecured interests and
ignored ethical custom press once more, the
philosophical jurist, called on to give a rational
account of creative juristic activity to secure
those interests and make materials of ethical custom and ethical speculation into legal materials,
turns back to the subordination of jurisprudence
to ethics and gives us new versions thereof.[44]

---

[44] A like movement is observable in politics: "There gradually
developed from this idea (Jhering's making interests the crucial
point rather than will) the important principle that the law dis-
closes a judgment of value concerning interests, that in this
judgment the moral nature of man is expressed, and that, as a

Perhaps what the new tendency comes to is this: Jurisprudence and legislation may not be separated by any hard and fast line and both presuppose political and social ethics.

We have now completed a survey of the three ways of looking at the relation of law and morals which obtained in the last century. We have traced the pedigree of each. We have seen the connection of each with the problems of some particular stage of legal development and how the hypothesis that was first used for a philosophical solution has changed its content continually in the long history of discussion of this subject, as the phenomena changed which philosophers were called on to explain, and yet has retained in substance the same name throughout. We have seen that no theory has been able to maintain itself, so that after twenty-four hundred years of philosophical and juristic discussion we are substantially where we began. If we said that to the analytical jurist law was law by enactment, that to the historical jurist it was law by convention, and that to the philosophical jurist it was law by nature, we should do the cardinal juristic doc-

consequence, lawmaking is not primarily a juridical but an ethical process." Krabbe, *The Modern Idea of the State* (transl. by Sabine and Shepard) 133. Hobhouse, *Elements of Social Justice,* subordinates politics to ethics.

trines of the last century no injustice and should
be putting them in terms that would be entirely
intelligible to a Greek philosopher. Moreover, he
would perceive that we were still debating the
questions he debated and that at bottom we had
made little progress with them. Even the endeavor of the mechanical sociologists to put the
matter wholly in terms of ethical custom would
seem to him, and seem rightly, but a way of saying that law was law by convention.

If, then, this protracted discussion appears to
have achieved no more than to demonstrate the
power of Greek thought to penetrate to the root
of a subject and grasp its fundamental difficulties, must we not conclude that we have been
pursuing a wrong method? May we expect to
understand social control or law as an agency of
social control by putting a question as to some
single simple relation and giving a single simple
answer? Social, and hence legal, phenomena do
not admit of simple explanations. Except for convenience of exposition, there are no such analytical lines as we have been seeking so persist-
ently to draw. Except for pedagogic purposes it
is impossible to lay out separate social sciences
with exactly limited frontiers, with customs
guards along the frontiers to prevent smuggling

of ideas across the lines, and standing armies to defend against invasion of the territory of one by another. Indeed one may suspect that the exigencies of academic teaching do not demand such limitations and that an academic predisposition to schematism is in part responsible. At any rate, these academic schematic layings out of the field of the social sciences eliminate too much of the whole and too much of each definite area which they set off from the whole. Even in such a matter as the relation of law and morals, the mere statement of the problem in this way eliminates too much.

If we look at the details of our own Anglo-American legal system with respect to their origin, we shall find that some rules and some principles were borrowed at one time or another from the Roman law, under a theory that Roman law had universal authority, or later under a theory that Roman law was embodied reason. But of these borrowed precepts, we shall find that some were traditional in Roman administration of justice, some were Roman scientific juristic generalizations, some were Greek philosophical speculations taken over by Roman jurists and applied to legal problems. We shall find other precepts were borrowed or assimilated from the canon law, and these again will be found to have diverse or composite origins. Roman law, texts of the Bible, writings of the fathers of the church and Germanic customary law contributed in varying proportions to precepts of the canon law which are now made into the body of American law. We shall find other precepts made by applying analogies of feudal society. Thus our whole mode of thought in terms of relation rather than of will, which differentiates Anglo-American law from the law of Continental Europe, is due to judicial treatment of all manner of questions, at the time when the common law was formative, on the analogy of the most conspicuous institution of that time, namely, the feudal relation of lord and man. Likewise the analogy of joint tenants of land fixed our ideas as to plurality of debtors and of creditors and makes us look at that situation very differently from Continental Europe, where the legal conception thereof goes back to the analogy of an undivided inheritance.

Pursuing our investigation, we shall find rules and institutions that are derived from Germanic customary law. We shall find other precepts and doctrines which are but judicial adaptations of medieval scholastic subtleties. We shall find sometimes judicial adoptions and technical workings over of customs of popular action, as in American mining law. We shall find a certain amount of adaptation of ethical custom. We shall find many precepts and doctrines which have their origin in reasoned systematic deductions of a technical legal science. For instance, in American procedure, we shall find the courts setting up a system of actions *ex contractu* and actions *ex delicto,* actions known neither to the common law nor to the codes of procedure, on the basis of a "natural" system of common-law actions worked out by text writers for convenience of exposition.[45] We shall find philosophical pictures of an ideal social order, as in American applications of the doctrine that the common law is in force only so far as "applicable." We shall find principles of abstract ethical speculation transformed into legal precepts, as in the case of more than one ultra-ethical doctrine of equity. We shall find scientific economic ideas used to fill out the content of abstract legal formulas, as when Mr. Justice Field, in applying the Fourteenth Amendment, turned to Adam Smith and thus gave us the conception of a legal right to pursue a naturally lawful calling, with a content derived from

---

[45] See Bliss, *Code Pleading,* § 9; *Supervisors* v. *Decker,* 30 Wis. 624; Scott, *Progress of the Law—Civil Procedure,* 33 Harvard Law Rev. 236, 240-242.

classical political economy.[46] We shall find scientific political ideas used in the same way in many legal precepts involving the idea of "sovereignty." Scientific academic technique and traditional professional technique will account for much. Ethical philosophy, economic theory and political ideas, both directly and indirectly in that compound which we call "public opinion," will account for much more.

When so many heterogeneous elements enter into the discovering and making and shaping and applying of legal precepts, and thus enter into the very legal materials themselves, we cannot bring the matter down to anything so simple as the relation of law and morals.

In general law cannot depart far from ethical custom nor lag far behind it. For law does not enforce itself. Its machinery must be set in motion and kept in motion and guided in its motion by individual human beings; and there must be something more than the abstract content of the legal precept to move these human beings to act and to direct their action. Yet one need but look at a mass of legal precepts that make up the bulk of legal systems today in order to see that they are anything but authoritative

---

[46] *Butchers' Union Co. v. Crescent City Co.*, 111 U. S. 746, 756-757.

promulgations of ethical custom. For the n.ost part they represent juristic or judicial search for a rule that will follow logically from the traditional legal materials, or for a rule that may be said to have authority behind it. They are technical workings over of the traditional precepts, or technical adaptations of authoritative extra-legal propositions. They are the technical, scientific custom of the courts and lawyers.

While jurists have been arguing the relation of jurisprudence and ethics, others have been urging upon them the relation of jurisprudence and economics, the relation of jurisprudence and politics and the relation of jurisprudence and sociology. Indeed one could say on each of these subjects much that has been said as to law and morals and could reach much the same result. Jurisprudence, ethics, economics, politics, and sociology are distinct enough at the core, but shade out into each other. When we look at the core or chiefly at the core, the analytical distinctions are sound enough. But we shall not understand even that core, and much less the debatable ground beyond, unless we are prepared to make continual deep incursions from each into each of the others. All the social sciences must be co-workers, and emphatically all must be co-workers with jurisprudence. When we set off a bit of social control and define its bounds by analytical criteria and essay to study it by its own light and with its own materials and its own methods exclusively, our results, however logical in appearance, are as arbitrary and as futile for any but theoretical purposes, as the division of the body of the defaulting debtor among his co-creditors in primitive law. The whole body could not be held by each; therefore a surgical operation was required to divide it among them.

BIBLIOGRAPHY

I

HISTORICAL

Bergbohm, *Jurisprudenz und Rechtsphilosophie,* 1892. pp. 251-276, 443.

An account and critique of various modern ethical systems of natural law.

Carter, *Law; Its Origin, Growth and Function,* 1907. Lects. 5, 6.

"Law begins as the product of the automatic action of society, and becomes in time a cause of the continued growth and perfection of society. Society cannot exist without it, or exist without producing it. . . . Law, therefore, is self-created and self-existent." 129

"Customs . . . being common modes of action, are the unerring evidence of common thought and belief, and as they are the joint product of the thoughts of all, each one has his own share in forming them. In the enforcement of a rule thus formed no one can complain, for it is the only rule which can be framed which gives equal expression to the voice of each. It restrains only so far as all agree that restraint is necessary. It is the reign of liberty, for it gives to each individual the largest possible area in which he can move and act with unrestricted freedom." 143.

Clark, *Practical Jurisprudence,* 1883. pp. 188-195.

Clark, *Roman Private Law: Jurisprudence,* 1914.
I, 22-23, 93-146 (§ 3).

A critique of Austin from the standpoint of historical
jurisprudence.

Holmes, *The Common Law,* 1881. Lect. 4.
Holmes, *Collected Papers,* 1920. pp. 168-179
(reprint of an address written in 1897).
Jenks, *Law and Politics in the Middle Ages,* 1898.
Chap. 8.
Jhering, *Geist des römischen Rechts,* (5 ed.)
1894. II, § 26.

Brings out the sharp line between law and morals in
the strict law.

Lightwood, *The Nature of Positive Law,* 1883.
Chap. 14.

"Even, then, before there is any necessity for a legal
sanction, we are able to assign perfectly distinct spheres
to morality, to law, and to the individual will. So long,
indeed, as morality and law exist in custom only, it is
difficult to distinguish them, but when once they come to
be expressed as rules, the distinction which I have been
pointing out begins to be apparent." 382.

Maine, *Ancient Law,* 1861, new ed. by Pollock,
1906. Chaps. 3, 4, 9.
Maine, *Early History of Institutions,* 1874. Lect.
13.

Pomeroy, *Introduction to Municipal Law,* 1864. §§ 10-14.

"The municipal law, as actually administered in Europe and America, is composed of ethics and history." 7.

Pouhaër, *Essai sur l'histoire générale du droit,* 1849. Chaps. 2, 3.

Puchta, *Cursus der Institutionen,* 1841 (transl. in part in Hastie, *Outlines of Jurisprudence,* 1887) I, § 7; (Hastie, 17-20).

"The jural and the moral view of a relation, when one of them is set up as exclusively valid, must assume a hostile attitude towards each other." Hastie, 17.

Pulszky, *Theory of Law and Civil Society,* 1888. pp. 316-332.

Savigny, *Vom Beruf unsrer Zeit für Gesetzgebung und Rechtswissenschaft,* 1814, (3 ed. 1840), reprinted 1892, (transl. by Hayward as "The Vocation of our Age for Legislation and Jurisprudence," 1831).

Chap. 2. The classical statement of the doctrine of the nineteenth century historical school.

A good account of this tract may be found in Small, *"The Thibaut-Savigny Controversy,"* 28 *American Journal of Sociology,* 711-734.

Savigny, *System des heutigen römischen Rechts,* 1840. I, § 7.

Schmoller, *Ueber einige Grundfragen des Rechts und der Volkswirtschaft,* 1875.   pp. 31-52.

Historical-economic.

Vinogradoff, *Common Sense in Law,* 1914. pp. 25-27, 56-60.

"Law is clearly distinguishable from morality. The object of law is the submission of the individual to the will of organized society, while the tendency of morality is to subject the individual to the dictates of his own conscience."   58.

Vinogradoff, *Historical Jurisprudence,* I, Introduction, 1920.   pp. 43-52.

Kantian.

II

ANALYTICAL

Adams, *Centralization and the Law,* 1906.   Lect. I.

Mechanical sociological-analytical.

"In the abstract, right and justice, as something beyond social convenience or, if you please, class advantage, are figments of the imagination. What you have, as a scientific fact, is an automatic conflict of forces reaching, along the paths of least resistance, a result favorable to the dominant energy."   35.

Amos, *Systematic View of the Science of Jurisprudence,* 1872.   pp. 77-78, 393-395, 514-516.

Amos, *Science of Law,* 1874.   Chap. 3.

"Not only are law and morality different, but they are the complement and, as it were, the very antitheses of one another." 32.

Austin, *Jurisprudence* (5 ed.) 1911.   The first six lectures were published in 1832.   Lect. 5.

The classical exposition of the analytical theory.

Bierling, *Kritik der juristischen Grundbegriffe,* 1877.   I, § 110.

Bierling, *Juristische Prinzipienlehre,* I, 1894. pp. 68-70.

Brown, *The Austinian Theory of Law,* 1906. pp. 34-55.

A critique and exposition of Austin.

Capitant, *Introduction à l'étude du droit civil* (3 ed.) 1912.   pp. 3-4.

Social organization rests equally on law and morals. The precepts of both are obligatory; those of law are enforced by public authority, those of morals are addressed only to the individual conscience.

Dillon, *Laws and Jurisprudence of England and America,* 1894.   pp. 11-20.

Gareis, *Encyklopädie und Methodologie der Rechtswissenschaft,* 1887, (5 ed. by Wenger,

1920; 3 ed. transl. by Kocourek as "Introduction to the Science of Law" 1911) § 6, Kocourek's transl. 38-42.

Goadby, *Introduction to the Study of Law,* 1910 (2 ed. 1914). Chap. 2.

Gray, *Nature and Sources of the Law,* 1909 (2 ed. 1921), §§ 642-657 (2 ed., 302-309).

Hearn, *Theory of Legal Duties and Rights,* 1883.

"Law is . . . the result of many factors. Among these factors each of the forces I have mentioned—the sentiment of justice, the conviction of utility, the force of custom—holds a prominent place. If justice be not the basis of all our law, it is the basis of that great body of law which determines the reciprocal duties and rights of men in their mutual dealings. . . . But justice has no place in determining the wants and the wishes of the state. These are matters of policy and discretion, constantly shifting, just as the wants and the wishes of individuals shift according to the circumstances of the case. It is in this part of our legal system that the principle of utility finds scope. . . . My present contention is that absolute duties rest mainly upon expediency and obligations upon justice; and that general duties, since they relate partly to public policy and partly to private right, are governed, not by one of these principles exclusively, but by both. It must not, however, be forgotten that in these complex affairs no force acts altogether apart from other forces, and that reaction and interaction are in constant operation." 70-71.

Holland, *Elements of Jurisprudence,* 1880 (12 ed. 1917). 12 ed. 29-40.

"The business of the jurist is, in the first place, to accept as an undoubted fact the existence of moral principles in the world, differing in many particulars in different nations and at different epochs, but having certain broad resemblances; and, in the second place, to observe the sort of sanction by which these principles are made effective. He will then be in a position to draw unswervingly the line which divides such moral laws from the laws which are the subjects of his proper science." 12 ed. 30.

Korkunov, *General Theory of Law,* (transl. by Hastings, 1909, 2 ed. 1922). First ed. in Russian, 1887; the translation is from the 6th ed., 1904. §§ 5-7.

"Thus the distinction between morals and law can be formulated very simply. Morality furnishes the criterion for the proper evaluation of our interests; law marks out the limits within which they ought to be confined." 1 ed. 52.

Markby, *Elements of Law,* 1870 (6 ed. 1905) §§ 12-30.

Nicol-Speyer, *Systematische Theorie des heutigen Rechts,* 1911. I, 196-208.

Analytical social-utilitarian.

Pollock, *Essays in Jurisprudence and Ethics,* 1882. pp. 18-30.

A critique of Lorimer's Institutes of Law from the analytical standpoint.

Pollock, *Oxford Lectures,* 1890. pp. 13-17.

A critique of metaphysical jurisprudence of the nineteenth century as "ethical jurisprudence."

Pollock, *First Book of Jurisprudence,* 1898 (4 ed. 1918). 4 ed. pp. 46-56.

"Though much ground is common to both, the subject matter of law and of ethics is not the same. The field of legal rules of conduct does not coincide with that of moral rules, and is not included in it; and the purposes for which they exist are distinct." 4 ed. 46.

Pollock, *Essays in the Law,* 1922. pp. 68-79.

A discussion of natural law in common-law decision and in the administration of justice in the British empire.

Rattigan, *Science of Jurisprudence* (3 ed.) 1899. pp. 3-11.

Roguin, *La règle de droit,* 1889. pp. 101-107.

Salmond, *First Principles of Jurisprudence,* 1893. Chap. 1, especially §§ 14-18.

A critique of the analytical view as to law and morals.

Salmond, *Jurisprudence,* 1902 (6 ed. 1920). § 72.

"Every right corresponds to a rule of right from which it proceeds, and it is from this source that it derives its name. That I have a right to a thing means that it is right that I should have that thing." 6 ed. 182.

Stone, *Law and its Administration,* 1915. Lect. 2.

Woodruff, *Introduction to the Study of Law,* 1898. pp. 4-7.

III

Philosophical

Abate Longo, *Filosofia del diritto,* 1885. I, 18-19.

Ethics is the common foundation. Morals regard man with respect to his ultimate destiny; law regards him with respect to the conditionally good in an external social relation.

Abbot, *Justice and the Modern Law,* 1913. Chap. I.

Historico-metaphysical.

"Legal obligation rests upon ethical obligation." 3.

Acollas, *Introduction à l'étude du droit,* 1885.

Neo-Rousseauist natural law. Attacks the historical school.

Acollas, *L'idée du droit* (2 ed.) 1889. pp. 9-10.

"For men precepts *(lois)* are of two kinds. Both have for their end human nature, for their organ reason, for their sanction conscience. They differ in that the domain of the one tends to increase and that of the other to diminish, since conscience, the sole sanction of the one, gets from the other the supplement of an external and social constraint. The former make up the science of morals, the latter the science of law. . . . Law is founded wholly upon freedom."

Ahrens, *Cours de droit naturel,* 1837 (8 ed. 1892). 8 ed. I, § 21.

Ahrens, *Juristische Encyklopädie,* 1855. pp. 35-39.

Arndts, *Juristische Encyklopädie,* (2 ed. 1850). 10 ed. by Grueber, 1901, § 13.

There are four points of difference: (1) In law man is considered as a person, i.e., because he has a free will; in morals we have to do with determining the will toward the good. (2) Law considers man only in so far as he lives in community with others; morals give a guide to lead him even if he were alone. (3) Law has to do with acts in so far as they operate externally; morals look to the intention—the inner determination and direction of the will. (4) Law governs the will so far as it may by external coercion; morals seek a free self-determination toward the good.

Baumgarten, *Die Wissenschaft vom Recht und ihre Methode,* 1920. I, §§ 1-12, especially § 10 (pp. 178-190).

Beaussire, *Les principes du droit,* 1888. pp. 24-30.

Kantian; much like the view of Amos, Science of Law, chap. 3.

Bélime, *Philosophie du droit,* 1855 (4 ed. 1881). I, 173-282.

Contrasts and distinguishes law and morals.

Binder, *Rechtsbegriff und Rechtsidee,* 1915. pp. 121 ff.

A critique of Stammler.

Boistel, *Cours de philosophie du droit,* 1899. I, §§ 30-39.

Follows the distinction made by Thomasius and shows how Pothier adopted the doctrine and even the terminology of Thomasius and has been followed by authoritative commentators on modern French law. pp. 64-65.

Bonnecase, *La notion de doitr en France au dix-neuvième siècle.* 1919.

A review of the different nineteenth-century theories.

Boucaud, *Qu'est-ce que le droit naturel,* 1906. Chap. 3.

Revived natural law.

Breuer, *Der Rechtsbegriff,* 1912. pp. 55 ff.

Says that Stammler's social science is a part of applied ethics.

Carle, *La vita del diritto* (2 ed.) 1890. §§ 280-283.

Metaphysical-psychological.

Cathrein, *Recht, Naturrecht und positives Recht,* 1901. 169-182.

Neo-scholastic.

Charmont, *La renaissance du droit naturel,* 1910. pp. 200-216. (Translated in *Modern French Legal Philosophy,* 133-145.)

Deals with the problem of legal precepts and the individual conscience.

Cogliolo, *Filosofia del diritto privato* (2 ed.) 1891. Bk. I, § 8.

Contrasts law and morals and argues a "complete separation between them." 113.

Cohen, *Jus naturale redivivum,* 1916.   Reprinted from 25 Philosophical Review, 761.

Courcelle-Seneuil, *Préparation à l'étude du droit,* 1887. Bk. 3.

Adopts Jellinek's theory of law as a minimum ethics. 203.

Cruet, *La vie du droit,* 1908.   pp. 86-179.

Positivist.

Dahn, *Vom Werden und Wesen des Rechts,* 1879. Reprinted in *Rechtsphilosophische Studien,* 291.   *Rechtsphilosophische Studien,* 305-306.

Ethics and law differ in principle.   Morality is the rational means of internal peace, while law is the rational means of external peace.

Del Vecchio, *The Formal Bases of Law,* (transl. by Lisle, 1914).   The part referred to is a

translation of Il concetto del diritto, 1906.   §§
96-111.

Seeks to unify law and morals (§§ 107-108).

"The truth of the alleged antinomy between law and
morals is this: that an act can be the object of diverse
judgments; and it can be weighed by individual criteria
different from those molded in positive institutions.
The antinomy does not exist between morals and law,
but between different ethical criteria; all of which, duly
applied, would give rise to a harmonious system of juridical values, and within every system the logical relations established would remain firm. We must remember, therefore, that law and morals are correlated ethical
categories, presupposing a common base."   § 108.

Demogue, *Les notions fondamentales du droit
privé,* 1911 pp. 13 ff., transl. in *Modern
French Legal Philosophy,* 365 ff.

Adopts Jellinek's view—see 13 n. 3.

"Law is that part of morals which seems to have such
importance that social forces, organized or not, ought to
make it their end to assure its application." 13.

Dewey and Tufts, *Ethics,* 1909. pp. 456-470,
especially 467-468.

Djuvara, *Le fondement du phénomène juridique,*
1913. §§ 93-99.

"Without going so far as to affirm with some authors
that the 'end of law' should be 'the realization of morals,'

for that would be an improper way of expressing oneself, one may say that that realization is implied by the idea of law—that it is one of its logical effects." 194.

Duguit, *L'état, le droit objectif et la loi positive,* 1901. (Transl. in Modern French Legal Philosophy.) pp. 101-105, (transl. 305-308.)

Law has its basis in social conduct. Morals goes on the intrinsic value of conduct. Hence it is vain to talk about law and morals. The legal criterion is not an ethical criterion.

Duguit, *Le droit social et le droit individuel* (2 ed.) 1911.

Introduction and lects. 1, 2.

Everett, *Moral Values,* 1918. pp. 309-312.

Fichte, *Grundlage des Naturrechts,* 1796, new ed. by Medicus, 1908, (transl. by Kroeger as *The Science of Rights,* 1889). See Medicus, *Fichte,* 1905, lect. 6.

"Fichte deduces his conception of *Recht* wholly without regard to the *Sittengesetz,* and he finds deep distinctions between morals and law. The *Sittengesetz* categorically demands that one do his duty; the rule of law only allows but does not command that one exercise his right." Medicus, 97.

Fowler and Wilson, *Principles of Morals,* 1894. II, 145-159.

Fragapane, *Il problema delle origini del diritto,* 1896. pp. 174-191.

Genetic-psychological.

Geny, *Méthode d'interprétation et sources en droit privé positif,* 1899 (2 ed. 1919). §§ 160-163 (2 ed. II, 93-113.)

Neo-scholastic.

Geny, *Science et technique en droit privé positif,* 1914, vol. III, 1921. I, §§ 13-20, II, §§ 141-159, especially 156.

Geyer, *Geschichte und System der Rechtsphilosophie,* 1863. pp. 3, 110-123.

Follows Herbart.
"Philosophy of law is a part of ethics." 1.

Green, *Principles of Political Obligation,* 1911. Reprint of lectures delivered 1879-1880. §§ 137-147, pp. 142-153.

Treats of the problem of conflict between the individual conscience and legal precepts.

Grueber, *Einführung in die Rechtswissenschaft,* 1907 (5 ed. 1919). pp. 19-30.

Gutberlet, *Ethik und Naturrecht,* (3 ed.) 1901. pp. 128-130.

Roman Catholic theological.

Law and right *(Recht)* cannot be separated from morality *(Sittlichkeit).*

Harms, *Begriff, Formen und Grundlegung der Rechtsphilosophie,* 1889. pp. 92-121.

"The territory of law is the moral world, and within this law has a definite place." 93.

Hasner, *Filosofie des Rechts,* 1851. §§ 48-49.

Contrasts law and morals.

Hauriou, *Principes de droit public* (2 ed.) 1916. pp. 7-17.

Metaphysical.

Heck, *Gesetzesauslegung und Interessenjurisprudenz,* 1914.

A critique of theories of interpretation and application of legal precepts.

Hegel, *Grundlinien der Philosophie des Rechts,* 1821 (ed. by Gans, 1840, ned ed. by Lasson, 1911). (Transl. by Dyde as *Hegel's Philosophy of Right,* 1896). See Reyburn, *The Ethical Theory of Hegel, A Study of the Philosophy of Right,* 1921. §§ 104-114.

Herbart, *Analytische Beleuchtung des Naturrechts und der Moral,* 1836. See Berolzheimer, *System der Rechts und Wirthschaftsphilosophie,* II, § 36, iv; *World's Legal Philosophies,* 248-252.

Ethics on a basis of psychology; philosophy of law a branch of ethics.

Herkless, *Jurisprudence,* 1901.   Chap. 6.

Hegelian.

Hildebrand, *Recht und Sitte auf den primitiveren wirthschaftlichen Kulturstufen* (2 ed.) 1907.

The relation of economic civilization to ethical custom and law.

Jellinek, *Die sozialethische Bedeutung von Recht, Unrecht und Strafe,* 1878 (2 ed. 1908).   Chaps. 1, 2.

Psychological, analytical, social-utilitarian.

Jhering, *Der Zweck im Recht,* 1877-1883 (4 ed. 1904).   The first volume is translated by Husik under the title, Law as a Means to an End, 1913.   Chap. 9 *(Das Sittliche),* the whole of vol. II.   See especially II, 189 ff.

The classical exposition of social utilitarianism.

Jouffroy, *Cours de droit naturel,* 1835 (5 ed. 1876).   Lect. 2.

Jung, *Das Problem des natürlichen Rechts,* 1912. §§ 3-5.

In the practical administration of justice, questions arise continually which cannot be solved by a smiple subsumption of states of fact under given legal precepts.   Out of the whole field of the ethical, law puts force behind certain duties which thus become legal duties.   Back of this is the ethical basis of right and law. The process is one of seeking to determine what is right and what wrong. § 10.

Kant, *Metaphysiche Anfangsgründe der Rechtslehre,* 1797 (2 ed. 1798). (Transl. by Hastie as Kant's Philosophy of Law, 1887). See Caird, *The Critical Philosophy of Immanuel Kant,* II, 292-350.

Kantorowicz, *Zur Lehre vom richtigen Recht,* 1909.

A critique of the Neo-Kantian theory of just law from a sociological standpoint.

Kirchmann, *Grundbegriffe des Rechts und der Moral,* 1869 (2 ed. 1873). See Sternberg, *Kirchmann und seine Kritik der Rechtswissenschaft,* 1908. 2 ed. 104-114.

A forerunner of social utilitarianism. Says that from the standpoint of jurisprudence, a right is desire plus power.

Kohler, *Rechtsphilosophie und Universalrechtsgeschichte,* in Holtzendorff, *Enzyklopädie der Rechtswissenschaft,* I, (6 ed. 1904, 7 ed. 1913). Not in prior editions. §§ 9, 10.

Kohler, *Einführung in die Rechtswissenschaft,* 1902 (5 ed. 1919). § 1.

From the historical-Neo-Hegelian standpoint. He recognizes a historical separation of law from ethical custom, the former having the force of politically organized society behind it. "The formation of morality as a higher order, above the legal order, ruling the individual not by a social compulsion, but by a religious precept or later through the power of an individual world-view, is a much later phenomenon."

Kohler, *Lehrbuch der Rechtsphilosophie,* 1908 (3 ed. by Athur Kohler, 1923). (The first edition transl. by Albrecht, as Kohler's *Philosophy of Law,* 1914).

Krause, *Abriss des Systemes der Philosophie des Rechtes,* 1828, enlarged and ed. by Röder as *System der Rechtsphilosophie,* 1874. *Abriss,* pp. 128-150.

Subordinates law to morals while contrasting them.

Krückmann, *Einführung in das Recht,* 1912. § 2.
Lasson, *System der Rechtsphilosophie,* 1882. §§ 23-25.

Hegelian.

Lioy, *Filosofia del diritto,* 1875-1880. (Transl. by Hastie from the third Italian edition as *Lioy's Philosophy of Right,* 1891).

Hastie's transl. I, 290-304.

Lorimer, *Institutes of Law* (2 ed.) 1880. pp. 353-367.

"The ultimate object of jurisprudence is the realization of the idea in the ideal of humanity, the attainment of human perfection, and this object is identical with the object of ethics. . . ."

"The proximate object of jurisprudence, the object which it seeks as a separate science, is liberty. But liberty, being the perfect relation between human beings, becomes a means towards the realization of their perfection as human beings. Hence jurisprudence, in realizing its special or proximate object, becomes a means towards the realization of the ultimate object which it has in common with ethics." 353-354.

Löwenstein, *Der Rechtsbegriff als Relationsbegriff,* 1915. pp. 39-68.

Criticizes Jellinek and Stammler.

Merkel, *Juristische Encyklopädie* (2 ed.) 1900. §§ 68-80.

Social-utilitarian.

Miceli, *Principii di filosofia del diritto,* 1914. §§ 90-92.

Psychological.

Miller, *Lectures on the Philosophy of Law,* 1884. Lect. 13.

Hegelian.

Miller, *The Data of Jurisprudence,* 1903. Chap. 6, "The Aim of Law."

Miraglia, *Comparative Legal Philosophy,* transl.
by Lisle, 1912, from the third Italian edition,
1903. Chap. 8.

Historico-metaphysical.

Niemeyer, *Recht und Sitte,* 1902.

Pagel, *Beiträge zur philosophischen Rechtslehre,*
1914. pp. 60-81.

Comments on Schuppe's theory.

Parsons, *Legal Doctrine and Social Progress,*
1911.

Soc˙al-utilitarian analytical.

Paulsen, *System of Ethics,* (transl. by Thilly,
1899.) pp. 599-638.

Phillipps, *Jurisprudence,* 1863. pp. 5-9.

"The science of morality comprises that of jurisprudence." 5.

Picard, *Le droit pur,* 1899, reprinted 1910. Bk.
9, *The End of Law; Justice.*

Socialist.

Radbruch, *Einführung in die Rechtswissenschaft,*
1910. pp. 7-13.

Substantially the same position as Jellinek.

Radbruch, *Grundzüge der Rechtsphilosophie,* 1914. pp. 74-81.

Relativist psychological social-utilitarian.

Rathkowski, *Encyklopädie der Rechts und Staats-wissenschaften,* 1890. §§ 8-47.

Röder, *Grundzüge des Naturrechts* (2 ed.) 1860. I, §§ 36-44.

Krausean. Compare Lorimer.

Rosmini-Serbati, *Filosofia del diritto* (2 ed.) 1865. I, 18-27.

Metaphysical, (Roman Catholic).

Rothe, *Traité de droit naturel,* 1885. I, 27-83.

Roman Catholic.

Schein, *Unsere Rechtsphilosophie und Juris-prudenz,* 1881. pp. 59-61.

Schuppe, *Grundzüge der Ethik und Rechtsphil-osophie,* 1881. pp. 282-292.

Smith, G. H., *Elements of Right and of the Law* (2 ed.) 1887. §§ 455-481.

A criticism of the analytical view as to law and morals, from the natural-law standpoint.

Smith, Munroe, *Jurisprudence,* 1908. pp. 6-14.

Social-philosophical. Distinguishes law and morals analytically.

Stahl, *Philosophie des Rechts,* 1829 (5 ed. 1878).
5 ed. II, 191-195.

A religious interpretation. Like the Roman Catholic jurists and the Herbartians, seeks to unify law and morals.

Stammler, *Wirthschaft und Recht,* 1896 (2 ed. 1905). §§ 31-33, 67-68, 95, 96, 99.
Neo-Kantian social-philosophical.

Stammler, *Lehre von dem richtigen Rechte,* 1902. pp. 21-32, 52-121, 146-168, 196-200, 285-291, 316-386, 447-496.
386, 447-496.

"All positive law is an endeavor to be just law." 31.

Stammler, *Wesen des Rechts und der Rechts-wissenschaft, in Systematische Rechtswissen-schaft* (Kultur der Gegenwart) 1906. pp. xviii-xxviii.

Stammler, *Theorie der Rechtswissenschaft,* 1911. pp. 437-558.

Stammler, *Lehrbuch der Rechtsphilosophie,* 1922.

Stampe, *Grundriss der Wertbewegungslehre,* 1912. I, 1-10.
Social-utilitarian.

Stephen, *Science of Ethics* (2 ed.) 1907. Chap. 4.

Sternberg, *Allgemeine Rechtslehre,* 1904. II, § 1.
Social-utilitarian.

Steudel, *Kritische Betrachtungen über die Rechtslehre,* 1884. pp. 162-171.

Review of theories of the relation of law to ethics
since Kant.

Stirling, Lectures on the Philosophy of Law,
1873. Lect. 3.

Hegelian.

Sturm, *Die psychologische Grundlage des Rechts,*
1910. § 22 (pp. 135-155).

Neo-Kantian. A critique of the biological-sociological
theory.

Tanon, *L'évolution du droit et la conscience so-
ciale,* (3 ed.) 1911. pp. 170-176.

Social-utilitarian.

Taparelli, *Saggio teoretico di diritto naturale,* (2
ed.) 1883. I, §§ 103-123.

Tissot, *Introduction philosophique à l'étude du
droit,* 1875. II, 228-271.

Metaphysical. Contrasts law and morals. See the
elaborate parallel, II, 252-255.

Tourtoulon, *Les principes philosophiques de l'histoire du droit,* 1919. (Transl. by Read as *Philosophy in the Development of Law,* 1922). II,
Chaps. 7, 14.

Trendelenburg, *Naturrecht auf dem Grunde der Ethik,* 1860 (2 ed. 1868). §§ 7-15.

"The separation of the legal from the moral, of the enacted from the ethically customary, which leads to the external formal legality of the Pharisees, must be given up. The false independence of juristic science, which was supposed to be a forward step, has not only distorted law in theory, but in the life of the law has divested it of its value, has furthered the setting up of a mechanism of law, and has taken the soul from the conception of law." 2 ed. 21.

Vareilles-Sommières, *Les principes fondamentaux du droit,* 1889.

Roman-Catholic natural law. Largely devoted to criticism of the doctrine of a natural right of revolution.

Wallaschek, *Studien zur Rechtsphilosophie,* 1889. pp. 52-63.

Watt, *An Outline of Legal Philosophy,* 1893. Chaps. 3, 11, 12.

Hegelian.

Whewell, *Elements of Morality* (4 ed.) 1862. pp. 209-230.

Wundt, *Ethics,* (transl. by Titchener and others, 1902-1907). I, 276-280; II, 135-136.

IV

SOCIOLOGICAL AND SOCIAL PSYCHOLOGICAL

Baldwin, *Social and Ethical Interpretations* (4 ed.) 1906. Chap. 15.

On conflict between the individual conscience and the law, see pp. 562-568.

Bonnucci, *L'orientazione psicologica dell' etica e della filosofia del diritto,* 1907.

Cardozo, *The Nature of the Judicial Process,* 1921. Lect. 2, "The Methods of History, Tradition, and Sociology;" Lect. 3, "The Method of Sociology: The Judge as a Legislator."

Cosentini, *Filosofia del diritto,* 1914.

General part, chap. 10, pp. 179 ff. Contains a good bibliography.

Coudert, *Certainty and Justice,* 1914. Chaps. 1-3.

An economic, class-interest interpretation.

"The truth is that the courts are constantly oscillating between a desire for certainty on the one hand and a desire for flexibility and conformity to present social standards upon the other. It is impossible that in a progressive society the law should be absolutely certain. It is equally impossible that the courts should render decisions conforming to the prevailing notions of equity without thereby causing a considerable degree of uncertainty, owing to the constant fluctuations in moral standards and their application to new and unforeseen conditions. New opinions are often due to economic changes, and many views regarding natural rights or individual liberty which were held fundamental in the last century sometimes find little support in the public opinion of the twentieth by reason of altered social and economic conditions." 12-13.

Ehrlich, *Grundlegung der Soziologie des Rechts,* 1913. Chap. 4.

The most important exposition of sociological jurisprudence.

Hobhouse, *Morals in Evolution,* 1906. I, Chap. 3.

Kornfeld, *Soziale Mächtverhaltnisse,* 1911. § 16.

The feeling of right as a source of law and an element in decision.

Lagorgette, *Le fondament du droit et de la morale,* 1907.

Social utilitarian.

Letelier, *Jenesis del derecho,* 1919. §§ 77-89.

Levi, *La société et l'ordre juridique,* 1911. Transl. from the Italian, published 1910. pp. 95-114, 184-193, 344-375.

Levi, *Contributi ad una teoria filosofica dell' ordine giuridica,* 1914. §§ 4-6, 22-24.

The relation of economics, law and morals: The consciousness of the individual ego—economics; of the social ego—law; of the autonomous ego—morality. So: individual valuation—economics; social valuation—law; universal valuation—morality.

McDougall, *Social Psychology*, (11 ed.) 1916. Chap. 15.

Oertmann, *Rechtsordnung und Verkehrssitte*, 1913. pp. 1-29.

Pontes de Miranda, *Systema de ciencia positiva do direito*, 1922. I, 391-426.

Post, *Die Grundlagen des Rechts*, 1884. § 3.

Biological-sociological.
"The ultimate foundations of law and morals are the same. Law is only a branch of morals in the wider sense." 18.

Rolin, *Prolégomènes à la science du droit*, 1911.

Psychological-sociological.

"In reality every legal precept corresponds to a rule of morals in course of evolution. As it succeeds, the legal precept tends to make the observance of the moral rule universal. If all legal precepts attained their end they would disappear and the law as a social phenomenon would perish with them." 124.

Ross, *Social Control*, 1904. Chap. 11.

Seitz, *Biologie des geschichtlich positiven Rechts*, 1906-1910. II, 439-460.

Biological-sociological.

Tarde, *Les transformations du droit,* 1894 (6 ed. 1909), chap. 6.

Psychological-sociological.

Vacca, *Il diritto sperimentale,* 1923. pp. 50-55, 163-189.

Vaccaro, *Le basi del diritto e dello stato,* 1893. Transl. as Les bases sociologiques de droit et de l'état, 1898. French transl. 446-459.

Biological-sociological.

Vander Eycken, *Méthode positive de l'interprétation juridique,* 1907. §§ 39-42, 115-124.

Vanni, *Lezioni di filosofia del diritto* (3 ed.) 1908. First publsihed 1901-1902. pp. 24-34.

Psychological-sociological.

Wurzel, *Das juristische Denken,* 1904. (Transl. in Science of Legal Method). pp. 62-66. Science of Legal Method, 371-377.

Psychological-sociological discussion of the influence of ethics on juristic and judicial thinking.

INDEX